Making Money in Thailand

A Retiree's Guide

Godfree Roberts, Ed.D.

ISBN:1482399636
ISBN-13:9781482399639

CONTENTS

My $7.50 Day

Living on a Budget

More Thai Language: The Best Thai Movies
With Subtitles

A Different Culture

CHAPTER 1: JUST DO IT

You'll find abundant business opportunities when you come to Thailand. The country is booming and its region, home to 550 million people, is developing rapidly. More than 22 million visitors will come to Thailand this year and, since Thais are unfamiliar with Westerners' tastes, there are many needs going unfilled.

And that's just the visitors. There is a much bigger market for unique (in terms of price, quality, or workmanship) world wide for Thai products. Thailand is not yet a big exporter, and the Thai Government offers considerable assistance to would-be exporters.

So come and take a look at the opportunities Thailand has to offer. You'll be pleasantly surprised at the lack of regulation, and the warmth with which your efforts are greeted. If you have any questions, write me or stop by. Then...just do it.

CHAPTER 2: HOW THAILAND WORKS

I've been making extra money since I retired to Thailand and I've met people who are making money here in ingenious ways. And they know people who know more ways. So I took each of them to my favorite lunch spot (they seemed to have all the time in the world: I never saw one of them glance at a watch) and asked them about making money in Thailand. If they didn't want to tell me their secrets would they tell me about someone they knew? After a few beers that they gave me enough advice and stories to fill a book that deals with four aspects of business in Thailand:

1. Thailand's Culture: How Thai people do business. Thailand's culture is completely different from ours, so please read Section 1 at least once. It will save you so much potential grief!
2. Internet Businesses. If you're happy in front of a computer screen for a few hours every day, then Internet businesses will be easier for you.
3. Real World Businesses: Starting and buying them. If you love meeting people and bustling around town then you'll enjoy Real World businesses.
4. Getting a Job in Thailand. If you want to play it safe and get a steady pay check, there's a job waiting for you. Before you make up your mind, read the whole book. You may be surprised.

My business is week-long, residential $1500 workshops for people interested in living here. I wrote another book, How to Retire in Thailand and Double Your Income, to help them decide if Thailand is a serious option for them. It describes Thailand's virtues and vices, what it takes and what it costs to live here. It explains how moving to Thailand doubles your effective income. It has budgets, prices, cultural guides, language instruction and everything except the experience of actually being here.

This book was written with a different purpose. Most workshop graduates who decided to stay in Thailand want to make extra money, and wanted much more information than we have time for in the workshops. This book is for people who want to live here and make money.

Let me know your own experience. Email me your criticisms, tips, corrections, and suggestions:
godfree@thailandretirementhelpers.com

Good luck with your new life, and stay in touch!

Godfree Roberts. Chiang Mai, Thailand, 2013

CHAPTER 3: BEFORE YOU LEAVE HOME

Before you leave home see if you can find a local business partner or associate. You may find a business idea in Thailand that requires someone back home to help make the Thai side work. Start by approaching your most reliable relatives and friends and discussing the idea in general terms. Set them and yourself up on Skype, and test it thoroughly before leaving home. Finally, update phone numbers, emails, Skype, and addresses of friends, relations and contacts.

Then ask yourself what companies in your area might benefit from either exporting to, or importing from, Thailand. Being an agent, intermediary, or broker is pleasant work. Thailand's economy is growing at 5.5%, and its 65 million people are open to new ideas and products.

Finally, review your life. What was your education? Your training? Career? Experience? Your most valuable contacts? Your keenest interests, hobbies, and passions? Draw up a list while you have the time. It will be very handy when you get here.

The best of both worlds is living in Thailand on a Western income. If you've retired then you have at least a $1200/month pension: sufficient for living in modest comfort. Since you'll have time on your hands and would probably like to start saving some money. Why not take advantages of Thailand's abundant opportunities and it's thriving economy? You're not swinging for the fences. All you're doing is

adding to your existing income.

Remember, you always have the choice to get the hell out of wherever you are and go somewhere else. And once you get to Thailand things will look very, very different. You'll be able to stop worrying about money. Once you relax you'll notice opportunities everywhere.

CHAPTER 4: THAILAND: AN INTRODUCTION

Business is business anywhere in the world. But doing business in a culture that's completely different to our own can be tricky. Thailand's ancient civilization has developed its own business procedures that are unlike anything we've ever seen. That's why this book begins with a description of the differences.

Why Learn the Language?

You're probably as lazy as me and would much rather skip the chore of learning a foreign language.

Even if you read this in the book, *How to Retire in Thailand and Double Your Income*, please re-read this advice on speaking Thai and understanding the culture, because doing business here is much easier if you speak the language and understand people's motivations. If you want to make money in Thailand, learning Thai is:

- Important
- Necessary
- Fun
- Profitable

You probably recognize the importance, even the necessity, of speaking the language of the people you're going to be dependent on.

So let's concentrate on the 'fun' and 'profitable' parts. I'm pretty laid

back about most of our workshop curriculum (this is Thailand after all) but learning the language is one thing I am pushy about. Here's why:

Most of us have comfortable life patterns and find the prospect of learning a new language daunting. Left to our own devices we might never get around to it. Living in Thailand, where few people speak English, without being able to understand anything being said or to express oneself, is like being in a silent movie. Tolerable for tourists,

but not for daily life.

Thais appreciate it. Really appreciate it. They can't wait to invite you for dinner, show you around, tell you about the kids - in other words, to include you in Thai life. Why exclude yourself from Thai life? If you have to talk to a policeman or an immigration officer and you use even a few Thai words you will find the whole meeting takes on a very friendly quality: Hey, this person has made an effort to speak our language.

And finally, imagine doing business where you live now and not speaking a word of English! You'd be awfully handicapped if you didn't understand the language.

Of course, your first few words will feel awkward, but don't worry. Thais will put you at ease. Just say the magic word (below) and they'll express astonishment at your linguistic proficiency, charm, good manners, and sophistication. They'll help you learn their language so that every meeting turns into a real social encounter (and a free language lesson).

Although the little 'language lessons' in this book may seem trivial, they're not. If you learn the half-dozen Thai words in these chapters, you'll win hearts wherever you go. Thais who "can't speak English", for example, will be emboldened by your efforts to suddenly start helping you...in English. So your modest efforts pay off in unexpected ways.

In addition to this spontaneous learning, our workshops also provide free online Thai lessons. And if they decide to settle here, we help graduates (we actually push them) to enroll in a Thai language class designed to overcome shyness, embarrassment or reluctance. We even have an expert who can teach you to read Thai in a week. So don't worry about the language. Once you take the plunge, you'll find 65 million charming people eager to help you.

A Delightful Way to Learn the Language – For Free

Another blessing that the Internet has brought us is free education.

MIT and Harvard have put all their courses and lectures on line so that anyone can study them – for free. And now you can have your own personal tutor to teach you Thai – for free. Seriously, how cool is that? Dickinson College has created Mixxer.com, a site to match up learners and teachers. In a few days you'll be matched up with a native Thai speaker who wants to learn English (or almost any language) in exchange for teaching you Thai. In the meantime, here are a few words that will take you a long way in Thailand.

The Magic Word

Here's some seriously good news: you only need one word to get around Thailand in style. And once you start using this magic word and see its effects you'll find it easy to add another and another:

The magic word? Khap (for men) and Kha (for women) It's pronounced like the long "a". Women tend to draw it out: khaaaa.

But how, you ask, could one word work so much magic? Well khap/kha has several meanings that are important in daily life.

You can use it to mean both 'please' and 'thank you'. So if you want something you can point to it and smile and say kha/khap and you will be considered polite and knowledgeable. And if you say it to the

Thai Airlines stewardess when she brings you a drink, it means 'thank you' – and she'll be charmed.

It can even be used to mean things like 'hello' and 'goodbye'. And it can be pushed to mean things like 'excuse me'. In fact, it is the WD-40 of social life in Thailand: it lubricates everything.

Listen for it when you're watching the Thai movies I recommend below and you'll get a feeling for it.

Peoples' Names

When you are introduced to a Thai you will make an interesting discovery: Thais are usually introduced only by their nicknames, and you will never discover their real names unless you ask. They also assume that Westerners cannot pronounce or remember long Thai names like former Thai Miss World, Lada Engchawadechasilp.

Thais don't go by their 'real' names. They're known almost exclusively by their childhood nicknames. The nickname can be preceded by khun, which is funny, because khun is a formal honorific, meaning Mister or Miss.

Of course, in formal or polite speech Thais will address each other by their given names, again preceded by khun. So Lada would be addressed at a formal event as "Khun Engchawadechasilp." But to her friends she would be 'Lek' (little one), her childhood nickname. If we met her at a party, she would be introduced to us as Khun Lek – 'Miss Little One'.

The chue-len (Thai *ชื่อเล่น*) "play-name" is given by parents or relatives in early childhood, these nicknames are typically one syllable. They may often be nonsense words or humorous, and usually have no relation to the person's actual name.

Some Thais also have second nicknames given at school, often linked to a notable physical feature or behavior. A boy who wears glasses may be called "Waen" (Thai: แว่น "glasses"). He may at some point adopt it as another nickname, even though he still uses his family-given nickname with family members. In other words, it is common for Thais to use three names: their family-given nickname, their school friends-given nickname, and the name on their birth certificate.

Understanding Thailand's Culture

Westerners and Asians have very different mindsets, and approach things from different perspectives. Since the failure to understand these differences often leads to misunderstanding, mistrust, and heartbreak, it's wise to learn about them now. If you read this in my first book, *How to Retire in Thailand and Double Your Income*, please re-read it here too. Understanding it will directly affect your earning power in Thailand.

Here's a summary of the differences from *The Geography of Thought: How Asians and Westerners Think Differently...and Why*, by Richard E. Nisbett. I urge you to read the whole book if you are serious about doing business here. Here are some assumptions we've all made, even without thinking about them:

Everyone has the same basic cognitive processes. Maori herders, Kung hunter-gatherers, and dot-com entrepreneurs all rely on the same tools for perception, memory, causal analysis, categorization, and inference.

When people in one culture differ from those in another in their beliefs, it can't be because they have different cognitive processes, but because they are exposed to different aspects of the world, or because they have been taught different things.

"Higher order" processes of reasoning rest on the formal rules of logic: for example a proposition can't be both true and false.

Reasoning is separate from what is reasoned about. The same process can be used to think about utterly different things and a given thing can be reasoned about using any number of different procedures.

All wrong! Asians' attitudes, training, culture, and habits allow them to successfully break all these 'universal' rules. It turns out that there's nothing universal about them: they're just our Western habits.

East Doesn't Meet West

Since Asian cultures are thousands of years old and since they recently avoided the Great Financial Crisis we've begun to wonder if their approach might be worth studying. When you get here you'll have ample opportunity to see how things are done. In the meantime, here are some clues gleaned from **The Geography of Thought:**

Law: The goal in Eastern conflict resolution is more likely to be hostility-reduction; compromise is assumed to be the likely result. Westerners call on universal principles of justice to push their goals, and judges and juries feel obligated to make decisions that they believe to hold true for everyone in approximately the same circumstances.

Debate: Japanese managers tend to deal with conflict with other managers by simple avoidance of the situation, whereas Americans are far more likely to attempt persuasion. What is intrusive and dangerous in the East is considered a means for getting at the truth in the West. Westerners place and almost religious faith in the free marketplace of ideas. Bad ideas are no threat, at least over the long run, because they will be seen for what they are and can be discussed in public. There has never been such an assumption in the East and there is not today.

Contracts: To us, a deal is a deal. Contracts are sacred. In the East, agreements are treated as tentative guides for the future. Contracts should therefore be reviewed whenever either party's circumstances change. This makes for much better long-term relationship, even at

the expense of short-term profits.

International Relations: To people in the East causation is never black and white or one-sided. Everything is interrelated, so they see things holistically. Rather than trying to see who is 'guilty' or 'wrong', they look to assign responsibility to both parties. Maybe not equally, but our phrase, "It takes two to tango" expresses their attitude.

Human Rights: Westerners think that individuals are separate, autonomous actors, and they enter into contracts with with one another and with the state that entails clear rights, freedoms, and duties. But East Asians see people as components of a culture, as parts of a much more important whole. So individual rights are minor compared to individual responsibilities to society. It's an entirely different concept of what an individual is.

Understanding Thailand's Business Culture

Thailand's culture is based on win-win outcomes. Nobody loses face. Everybody leaves smiling.

So Thai merchants look beyond mere transactions and seek to build

relationships. They have a longer time horizon than us, as you would expect in an ancient culture.

Western negotiators see the business process as competitive, whereas Thais regard negotiation as a cooperative undertaking that develops over time. We want substantive outcomes; they're working toward relational outcomes.

Relationships mean repeat business. And any merchant will tell you that repeat customers are more valuable because the cost of acquiring them and learning their quirks and peculiarities is zero. They're also more likely to forgive you if you screw up.

If you find a successful product here you will become dependent upon your supplier, so you want to lay a foundation of mutual trust and respect from the very first meeting. THAIS NEGOTIATE BASED ON RELATIONSHIP. RELATIONSHIP COMES FIRST. ALWAYS.

Another important difference is Thais' expectation that a signed deal is the beginning of something, not the end. There is no such thing as a "fixed" contract in Thailand (or anywhere in Asia, for that matter). Contrary to what many Westerners think, this does not mean that Oriental people are 'slippery' or 'untrustworthy'. Quite the contrary.

A win-win, long-term relationship means that, if conditions change the parties to the deal will be able to sit down and make adjustments to the terms of the original contract. It's a matter of give and take. Sometimes you'll find yourself on the giving end. Sometimes you'll be the grateful taker. Relax and go with the flow. Part of the reason you're living in Thailand is to participate in a new culture. It's fun!

Business Demeanor in Thailand

Thailand is a non-confrontational society. Avoid public disputes and criticisms at all costs. And never use ironic humor. It's neither understood not appreciated. From Thais' point of view, openly criticizing someone is little different from slapping them in the face. They view it as a deliberate attempt to offend and harm the person

you are criticizing.

Open anger (usually caused by Westerners' lack of cultural awareness or language skill) betrays a spiritual failure and risks attracting negative spirits, which bring violence and tragedy with them.

Since Thailand is a close-knit, hierarchical society, for a Thai to lose face is a near-tragedy. Never, ever do anything to cause a Thai to lose face. Always look for a compromise, or a different approach to accomplishing your objective. Or just walk away.

Always leave the other party a way to avoid loss of face. If you forget this just lose face yourself. Surprisingly, you gain status with Thais for doing so – especially if you are in the right. Your own ability to lose face gracefully will (though it looks strange to our eyes) raise your status among Thais. There is no disgrace – and often real gain – in deliberately losing face.

Thais emphasize and value outward forms of courtesy such as politeness, respect, genial demeanor and self-control. They value harmonious relations far more than Westerners do.

Business Meeting Etiquette

Like most people Thais prefer doing business with someone they respect. But this goes beyond mere preference: it is hugely important in Thai business. In case you have a formal business meeting in Thailand here are a few tips for earning that respect:

One meeting does not create a relationship. Relationships develop

slowly so it may take several meetings before you are ready to do 'real' business.

Even though this is true everywhere, in Thailand you should always be respectful and courteous when dealing with others. This leads to the necessary harmonious business relationships.

With Thais, communication is formal. Non-verbal communications often mean more than verbal communication: the way you carry

yourself, bow, or smile are all closely observed.

Thais have great difficulty saying 'no', so be sensitive to their non-verbal communication of reluctance or embarrassment.

By the same token, watch your own body language and facial expressions as Thais will believe them more than your words.

Show respect by always making appointments a month in advance (if you cannot, apologize for rushing things). This says to the person you're dealing with, "I realize that you are an important person with a busy schedule, and I'd be grateful if you could fit me in a month from now."

Once you've made a formal appointment, follow it up with a confirming letter giving your own qualifications and background, as well as that of anyone who will accompany you. This helps your Thai host know how to introduce you correctly – a big deal here.

Punctuality, even though not a Thai virtue, is taken as a sign of respect when you show up for your appointment.

Dress as well as you can afford. And conservatively. You will be judged on your dress.

If you are going to make a proposal include an outline – in English and Thai – and as much detail as you can, with your letter of confirmation. This gives your host time to think it over and discuss it

with colleagues. Your meeting will make faster progress and save an extra visit.

Thailand is a hierarchical, Confucian society. Rank is always respected. The oldest person in the group is the most honored in terms of seating and deference to their opinion.

Remain standing while you are introduced and wait until you are shown where to sit. Thais are extremely sensitive to seating arrangements and, who knows, the Chairman of their company may be at your meeting and his status must be respected.

If it's a real business meeting, present your business card (in English on one side, Thai on the other) – using your right hand, while bowing – to everyone.

Be   patient.   Relax.   Enjoy   your   tea.

CHAPTER 5: STARTING A BUSINESS IN THAILAND

Wealth-seeking Expatriates Favor Asia: Survey

The world's wealth-seeking expatriates increasingly favor countries and regions in the Asia Pacific such as Singapore, Thailand and China's Hong Kong, a latest survey has found.

The survey on expatriate wealth, based on economic factors such as earning power, disposable income and ability to accumulate luxuries, also sees the Chinese mainland and Vietnam advancing to the top ten positions, said banking giant HSBC, who commissioned the Expat Explorer Economics survey.

The results of the survey released on Monday showed that 54 percent of the Singapore-based expatriates surveyed earn more than 200,000 U.S. dollars a year, compared to a global average of only 7 percent.

Four out of five expatriates in Singapore saw an increase in their disposable income since relocating here. About 44 percent reported an increase of 50 percent or more in their disposable income, compared to the global average of 19 percent.

Expatriates in places such as China's Hong Kong, Malaysia and the Chinese mainland also saw an increase in their disposable income since moving to these places.

The results of the survey was in line with the trend of Asia becoming a leading destination for expatriate earning potential amid the weak global economy. Whereas the Middle East has reigned in previous years as the destination of choice for expatriates seeking to increase their wealth.

Bermuda came in second as the best destination for expats seeking wealth.

Apart from Singapore, Thailand finished in the third place on the Expat Explorer Economics league, followed by China's Hong Kong in the fourth place. The Chinese mainland and Vietnam came in the 7th and 10th, respectively.

"We are now also seeing expatriate wealth heading to this region. Singapore especially, is fast becoming an all-round expatriate destination for career progression, financial rewards and quality of life," said Paul Arrowsmith, head of retail banking and wealth management at HSBC Singapore.

Singapore attracts high-flying, ambitious expatriates with strong career aspirations and who are internationally mobile. About 72 percent of expatriates in Singapore cited financial rewards as part of the reasons for them to move here, and 70 percent cited better job prospects, with 74 percent willing to consider moving to another expatriate posting after this one. (CRI English 10-09-2012)

So...

Several of my friends who are making money in Thailand suggest your first goal should be to make a profit of just $50 a week. As they explained, since you already have an income, setting a first goal of $50/week is wise for two reasons:

1. It gets you earning something in a brand new business. It breaks the ice without stressing you out to reach it.

2. It shows you just how much money $50/week is when it comes on top of your pension: $50/week is $2,500/year. $2500 will fly two of you home for Christmas – or to the Forbidden City in Beijing for a month.

Did you ever think you'd be considering a vacation in China . . . or at the Taj Mahal? They're only a few hours and a cheap ticket away from Thailand. Air travel is fiercely competitive in Asia, and therefore, cheap.

Laying the Foundation

Starting your own business in Thailand is much like starting a business anywhere and conforms to the same rules that have applied for thousands of years.

In other words, it takes about two years to become established, requires effort every day, and you can't go to sleep at night until you've done everything possible that day to make progress.

Oddly, this self-imposed discipline is also a lot of fun – especially when you're earning extra money and not struggling to survive. With your anxiety level low, you'll have the free energy and attention to handle the inevitable challenges and disappointments.

The steps described below will help you plan, prepare and manage your business. Click on any of the links to learn more.

⅄ **Step 1:** Write a Business Plan: You probably don't like planning any more than I do, but it can be really helpful. It's not so much a plan of action as a system for making us think about all the elements that go into a successful business.

⅄ **Step 2:** Get Business Assistance: There are all kinds of courses, many of them free, to help you become business-savvy. Unless you're about to jump on the plane for Thailand, take advantage of all your local free training and counseling services; from preparing a business plan, to securing financing, to expanding or locating a business. If you get one good, actionable idea from your investigation you're ahead of the game.

⅄ **Step 3:** Choose a Business Location: If you're going to start a home-based business then this is not an issue. Otherwise, get advice on how to select a customer-friendly location, which is the same in Thailand as it is anywhere. You'll be amused to hear that you won't have to comply with zoning laws in Thailand: there aren't any. But location is still as important here as it is anywhere else.

⅄ **Step 4:** Finance Your Business: This is not the time of life to be borrowing money. Nor is it likely that you can borrow money for a Thai-based business unless you have very trusting relatives. Besides, you'll need to speak pretty good Thai and understand the business and legal culture here before investing a penny. And that will take you at least a year of daily study. As you read more I think you may find it more attractive to start a business here that is not dependent on a physical location. You can create a new business on an income of just $1200/month if you live in Thailand. That's what I did, and you can see details of it later in the book.

⅄ **Step 5:** Understand Employer Responsibilities. If you're going to employ Thais (which the Thai government strongly encourages) learn the legal steps you need to take to hire them in Thailand. Local employers may play fast and loose with employee rights and benefits, but foreigners who do the same receive little sympathy from the authorities.

Will Your Business Be Profitable?

Here are three questions to ask yourself. Fortunately, you can test all of them before you lose any serious money:

1. Are there plenty of buyers? In other words, is there a sufficient number of people that you can affordably reach who will continue buying at least one item a day from you? This short video tells how: You can run tests, for free, on Amazon and eBay.

2. What are people willing to pay? There are people willing to pay 25¢ for practically anything. But are they willing to pay you $25 so that you can make a decent profit – after you've taken all your costs into account?

3. Is the market growing? The Internet is growing, which is a plus, but is your target market? Try to figure out the profile of your ideal customer in advance. We know, for example, that as Baby Boomers retire there'll be about 90 million of us in

the English-speaking world alone.

To find out the answers to these questions here are some useful tools:

Browse existing platforms. Warrior Forums and DigitalPoint are two discussion sites where you can see current products and marketing approaches. You can learn a lot there just by watching the discussion flows.

Ask your community and friends. Everyone you know (both real world and on line) with similar interests. What interests them? What are they willing to pay?

Piggyback: Write to email and online marketers who are selling something similar to your intended product. Ask if you can run a test mailing to, say, 1,000 people on their list.

Keyword Research Tools. Google's Adwords is a wonderful, free research tool that lets you play around with all the possible search terms that people might use to find a product like yours. It's flexible and fun. If there are 368,000 people searching for 'Thai silver jewelry' every month then at least you know that there's a big market for it and, if your product is a unique example of Thai silver jewelry, your chances are good.

Soft Launches: These are also called 'limited' launches. Set up a complete, free sales page on either eBay or Amazon for your product. See how many people click on it, and how many click through to the sales page. On the sales page you can have a message saying that you are temporarily sold out but, if they leave their email address you'll get back to them when the item comes into stock. This way you will quickly and cheaply discover just how much interest there is for your product.

CHAPTER 6: AN ENTREPRENEUR IN THAILAND

American Expat Greg Miller: "A Western expat in Thailand often has to think about making money. Thailand is a paradise in many ways, but if you don't have any money, it can be a hell.

Even if you're getting a steady pension check, social security or trust fund payout there is always the fear that the home currency can lose value against the Thai Baht, so it is important to find some kind of income stream locally. One of the ways to do that is to start your own business, but in Thailand there are special considerations that have to be taken into account.

First of all, being an entrepreneur is not for everyone. As compared to salaries, entrepreneurial incomes go up and down and there are always strange things that hit the business owner, making stress part of the price that must be paid. But that's the same everywhere. You have it, or you don't.

A foreigner can own only up to 49% of the equity of a corporation or partnership in Thailand (a Limited Company). That means there must be Thai partners who will own the majority. There are exceptions possible if you work through the Ministry of Commerce to set up a Foreign Business License, but these are typically granted

for companies starting out with large capitalizations that will employ a lot of Thais. An existing company that wants to set up manufacturing in Thailand for export would be a good candidate for that type of business license.

Even though she might have a minority of the equity, the expat can still maintain control if she designs the business so that she is the managing director, and so that no Thai partner has a large portion of the ownership. It is essential that a Western expat employ professional Thai accountants and a lawyer to set up the company here.

In order for an expat to work in a Thai corporation a work permit must be obtained (with fees), and four Thai nationals must be employed for every one foreigner working at the company. And once working with a permit, you must pay yourself a minimum of 50,000Baht per month (about $1650 USD) in taxable income.

There are businesses for sale in Thailand, but the same rules apply for the new expat buyer even with existing businesses.

I partnered with my wife (a Thai national) and a couple of her close Thai relatives to establish our corporation, originally designed as just a travel agency, Top Thai Travel, Ltd. Top Thai Travel offers tours within Thailand, and localized travel services such as local specialized tours, Thai cooking schools, Elephant Farm experiences, hotel reservations and domestic air tickets.

That worked well so we expanded the business to include a Thai restaurant, condo rentals for visitors to Chiang Mai, and a boutique fashion shop. Our main goal was to earn a little income while having fun Thai adventures and, in that regard, we have done very well. I found that actually establishing the corporation in Thailand was less cumbersome than back in the US, where we had to report to so many different redundant government agencies.

An alternative for entrepreneurs to the restrictions of setting up a Thai company is to establish a sole proprietorship in the home country (like in the US). One can work this way as a contractor, such as writing articles for websites or publishing an ebook, or as a small resale business, such as buying Thai products and exporting them back to your home market. A sole proprietorship puts things on a small scale, but also can be more flexible, with much of the work being done individually on a virtual basis.

A work permit requirement is enforced only if the work is involving a Thai company or directly competes with Thai companies. For instance, if you are a financial consultant that is employed by Thai companies you will likely need a work permit, and the same would be true if you operated a sole person travel agency serving foreigners visiting Thailand that competed with local Thai businesses.

But if you are trading US stocks on the computer or building websites for American shops online, you should not have to worry about getting a work permit or other documentation. The Thai laws in this regard are vague and are subject to local interpretation, but generally if you don't rock the boat for Thai businesses, you can probably work with little worry about permits.

These regulations allow expat entrepreneurs to get involved in a lot of small businesses that are independent and not interfering with the Thai marketplace. So for an expat to start up a little food cart businesses competing with Thai street vendors would be impossible. Establishing a restaurant with Thai partners and employing Thais as staff is doable – with a little planning and business set-up. Something like an independent computer consulting business for international clients from a home office is very easy to establish.

There are lots of expats in Thailand involved in exporting Thai products. Some sell directly online through websites like Amazon and eBay, or on a dedicated shopping website. That usually involves pretty hefty shipping charges added on to the products sold. To get around this many expat exporters partner up with someone in their home country to ship individual orders out to end users. Shipping a large amount via a container, or even a partial container that will base cost on a square meter basis, can be a lot more economical that sending out individual small shipments from Thailand.

Finding unique Thai products that will have a steady market back home is the trick. Some products that seem to do extremely well are Thai Buddha statues, hand woven silk and finely carved wood wall art. There is so much available from Thai artisans that it is not difficult to find something that is truly different from other mass produced products that will always be appreciated in the West.

I met an entrepreneur from Seattle who spent most of his time in Thailand raising orchids in the large greenhouse next to his home. The natural resources and gardening skills are plentiful in Thailand, and the climate is ideal for having product grow and developing unique colors and strains of the flowers.

Once a year he would head back to Seattle with a container load of the finest orchid plants one could find. Within a month back in his home country, he had it all sold with enough sales and profits to keep him going till the next trip.

The limitations for an entrepreneur in Thailand, like a self-employed person anywhere, is to develop a business that you can do well and that there will be a viable market while working under the Thai legal regulations. The more creative, hard-working and skilled enterprises will always be the successful one"s.

Good luck with yours! You can stay abreast of mine just be clicking on the link below and signing up for our free newsletter. Greg Miller, American Expat in Chiang Mai (Subscribe!)

CHAPTER 7: DOING EBAY FROM THAILAND

Rather than jumping in at the deep end of the Internet business world, why not start at the shallow end where everything is set up and waiting for you? As your confidence and ambition grows you can graduate to some of the more sophisticated programs described in the later chapters of this book. Because so much of what is true about eBay also applies to other online businesses, I'll go into detail here to save repeating information later in the book. eBay is a convenient choice because you already know how it works and because it involves real, tangible products. In the next chapter we'll talk about pure Internet businesses that you can run from Thailand or, for that matter, from anywhere.

eBay

Over 1,000,000 people make a full-time living on eBay, which is not surprising when you consider that eBay will have 80,000,000 unique visitors this month alone. Say that out loud: "Eighty million visitors this month". 80,000,000 people looking to buy something. So there's surely room for you on eBay.

Have you ever sold anything on eBay.com? If you're not familiar with eBay I strongly recommend a book: eBay for Seniors for Dummies (Amazon). It's part of the 'Dummies' series and is excellent.

If you've never sold there, do it right away. It's fun and easy. You can sell practically anything that's lying around the house. And if you decide to move to Thailand you can do what I did and sell the entire contents of your house on eBay. I paid for my air ticket and financed the writing and production of my first book, How to Retire in

Thailand and Double Your Income from the money I made on eBay.

Videos: Money Shots

You will need some basic equipment, especially a digital camera that's

suited to the kind of items you'll be selling. If they're small items then your camera has to be able to take tight closeups of them. A cheap tripod is also a good investment. Both can be had for a few hundred dollars.

For some good, free advice advice, enter product photography in YouTube. Then, if you're interested (it's fun and a professional-looking product shot is extremely important) make use of Scott Kelby, a one-man university system, who teaches photography through books, DVDs, streaming online photography courses, live seminars and iPad apps.

His latest app, Scott Kelby's Lighting Recipes , for the iPad, lets you audit a course for free. In the video, Scot demonstrates how he achieved 20 different shots through 13 lessons. The examples vary from studio glamour shots to outdoor sports portraits. The app shows a finished photo followed by a behind-the-scenes look at how the lighting effects were achieved, narrated by the lively Mr. Kelby.

If you don't have an iPad you can still make use of Scott's paid video photography course (requires Flash).

How eBay Works from Thailand

Assuming you've now got some photographs you're happy with and you know a little about eBay, let's look at how it works when you're selling products from abroad. All my successful eBay Thailand friends gave me very similar advice:

Find something here in Thailand – anything – that really attracts you. Something you've never seen back home that you would like to own or give to friends and relations. This natural attraction is important when you begin. As your experience grows you will use other criteria to choose products. Here are some of the many ways to start your personal treasure hunt:

Browsing a local supermarket (not a foreign-owned one) here you will be filled with wonder at things you never dreamed existed.

Attend some trade shows. Thailand is one of the trade show capitals of the world, and they're fun. See the trade show calendar at the end of this book for details.

Head for the hills. Thailand's many ethnic groups live in hilly areas and they have highly developed handicraft traditions. They would be thrilled to have a connection to the outside world. They'd much prefer to stay in their villages and sell to you than trudge miles to sell on the street in town. Since everything is hand made it's not difficult for them to make items to your precise specifications and size. This is fun because it gets you out into the remote countryside and ensures that the items are genuinely unique. At the same time you are helping sustain exotic cultures that would otherwise be destroyed through assimilation.

Research your first-choice product on eBay using the tools below. Is anyone selling it, or something like it? At what price? With what shipping terms? Your competitive analysis is important. If your first-choice product is already being offered at a competitive price, either drop it and move on, or ask the manufacturer to modify it for you so that your version is unique.

Watch how similar items perform. How many are offered? How quickly do they sell? How many bids? What are the shipping terms? Happily, eBay keeps track of all these things for you. Just use their "Watch This item" feature and it's done. If you use a smartphone or iPad (highly advisable) eBay has an app that is fast and easy to use, even here in faraway Thailand.

Make sure it's not too heavy or bulky for airmail shipment unless, of course, its value offsets its weight or bulk.

Find out where in Thailand that item is made or sold wholesale. The wholesale market in Chiang Mai, where I live, is down by the river. Stuff there is unbelievably cheap, and they do sell single items if a carton is more than you need. Don't worry about finding the original manufacturer yet. That comes after you've figured out if there's a market for it. There are several guides for finding manufacturers below.

Buy some (even one) from the nicest vendor. Don't haggle the first time. If you become a repeat buyer you can haggle, but you may not want to since you will be offered discounts and even freebies. Thai merchants understand the value of repeat customers and will strive to earn your loyalty.

Photograph it until you get several good, tight pictures. eBay encourages the use of multiple images and you'll want to show different angles. Make sure that the pictures show it to its best possible advantage. Be patient and persistent. This is the most important step after the product itself, so take your time.

Package it carefully for shipment to your intended market. Take it to the Thailand Post Office and ask them for three prices:

- Surface Mail
- Air Mail standard
- Air Mail with Thailand Post Office's Track & Trace

Now you know your shipping costs and can start figuring your strategy: Will you ship your products home in bulk and have your home-based partner handle in-country shipping? Will you sell it directly, with a "shipping extra" sign? Will you sell directly, add the shipping costs in to your selling price, and offer 'free shipping'?

A Product Suggestion

I spent months here looking for a chemical-free herbal shampoo since my scalp is allergic to synthetics. Back home when I had money I used to pay $12 a bottle for 11 oz. of Aubrey herbal shampoo at Whole Foods.

In Thailand I found an excellent herbal shampoo for 65 Baht ($2) in an expensive department store. You could buy it for $0.50 - $1 wholesale and sell it for $5 -$6 on line.

So opportunities lurk everywhere. In fact, just the range of novel products in your local Thai supermarket will start your mind racing. (And the website name www.thaiherbalcosmetics.com was available

when I wrote this).

Building Your eBay Empire in Thailand

Your first task is to find one successful product that sells one every day, month after month. An example of a successful product is one that sells for $20, costs you $5, and sells one per day.

A really successful product costs you $10 in Thailand and sells one a day for $79.95 back home. This ideal product represents an 8:1 markup and will earn you $2,100 gross profit every month.

If you want to sell Thai products you don't have to wait for trade shows. For clothes, you can just head down to Pratunam, the fashion area in Bangkok. The weekends are frantically busy, so go midweek. Spend a few pleasurable hours or days wandering around chatting with the merchants and manufacturers, picking up samples to photograph and test online.

Selling It

Your product will not sell itself. So your next task is to sell it. If you do nothing, your $10 product is still worth $10. Your job is to make people at home want to pay $80 for it – and to be really happy when they open the box. This means four things:

- ⅄ One. Photography
- ⅄ Two. Story
- ⅄ Three. Packaging
- ⅄ Four. Testing

Another Product Suggestion

Like millions of people, I'm into yoga. Women's yoga clothes (forget men's clothes, they're a waste of time) can be made here out of any fabric: Silk? Linen? Spandex? Cotton? To your design, very cheaply.

You can have them custom-embroidered (for either the individual or a yoga studio) for a few cents. Yoga bags, towels? Your own

complete line. You can ship them in plastic shipping envelopes.

Incidentally, the name, www.thailandyogaclothes.com is available as of this writing.

More About Photography: Because it's so important, read up on photographing products for eBay. If you carefully follow their directions your product will look better than 90% of your competition.

Story: There's much more to a good eBay product description than you'd think, especially since your products will be unique. A unique product, one that no-one has ever seen, means that you are asking potential customers to make a real leap of faith. Here are two excellent articles on-line to get you started: *How to Categorize and Describe Your eBay Products* and, for the more advanced, *How to Describe Items for Sale on eBay.*

Packaging: Paper, cardboard, design, and printing costs are low in Thailand and quality is high. For your ideal $79.95 product you might consider a custom box with beautiful, complementary wrapping. For your $20 product you may be able to afford a nice off-the-shelf box and tissue paper. Presentation makes a big difference, and you want to make the unwrapping process as delightful as possible, even if it means that your profit margin is lower. On eBay, good reviews and repeat business are more important than getting the highest possible profit from each item.

Testing. Testing: All my successful friends (the failures wouldn't admit they'd failed) told me how important it is to test everything.

Happily, eBay allows you to have multiple identities linked to your PayPal account. So you can sell the same item at different times – or even simultaneously under different names at different prices, or with different descriptions and photographs.

Since you are testing and not trying to make the most profit, you could offer free shipping, shipping at 99¢, and shipping at the regular price. As you can see, there's a lot to be learned about optimizing your eBay store, and it's fun to tweak it and get instant feedback in

the form of sales.

You can test your eBay product ideas before you spend any serious money, which is great for beginners. You can even test your product idea on eBay before you have the product. EBay for Dummies tells you how.

Failure is an Option!

Most people who start a business on eBay fail. They fail for the same reasons that most people who start any business fail. Happily for us, the simplicity of eBay makes it easier to avoid the major pitfalls. Since you're the boss of this business, the only person to blame for failure is you. So here is a quick summary of the reasons people are most likely to fail:

Preparation: Read everything you can get your hands on about eBay businesses. Join mailing lists, participate in on-line forums. Even go to classes to meet other successful eBay merchants. The first one I met was an insurance agent who sold just one insurance product on-line: an insurance 'wrapper' for people who wanted to insure their houses and who owned boats. A funny niche, but he worked from home and made a steady $100,000 net income year after year. I never forgot that.

Persistence: Most people give up too soon, and for the wrong reasons. Re-read the story of my friend who sells Thai children's clothes. She lost $200/week for a year while she tested potential products and prices.

Undercapitalization: Later in the book I tell the story of one of our graduates who is very successful selling on eBay. She invested $200/month from her savings until she found the right formula. Month after month, for 13 months, she watched her bank balance decline. So set realistic goals for how much you're able to afford to 'lose' each month. If you keep good records you're not losing a penny: you're investing.

Inflexibility: Some people keep doing the same thing over and over,

expecting a different result. So...if at first you don't succeed try, try a different variation. If your original idea was sound then tweak it until it works. If it wasn't sound, then scrap it and try something completely different.

Not Enough Testing: Or not enough variations tested. The eBay books and articles I recommended earlier will give you a ton of ideas about testing. Try them all until you really understand what's happening.

Not Seizing the Opportunity: At some point you will find a products that starts selling like crazy. (Perhaps it's that natural Thai herbal shampoo that cost you 50¢ and you're selling for $5, and everyone who visits eBay and sees it and thinks, "why not?").

At that point, stop testing and start selling! Run down to your supplier and buy 100 (or 1,000, or even 10,000) of them. Run back and place your ad again. Try a 'split' ad at $6. eBay makes this easy. It might drive more people to your $5 product because they now perceive $5 as even better value. Or maybe you sell just as many for $6. That's the fun of eBay. You can tweak it to your heart's content.

Poor Response to Customers: If you don't fill every order and respond to every email the same day you receive it, you're operationally mediocre. There are plenty of ways to be mediocre but this is #1.

If the logic of this statement isn't clear to you then eBay (and possibly any business) is not for you. Let me repeat: if you are serious about this business you will never, ever go to bed at night unless you have shipped every order, responded to every email, and handled every complaint patiently and generously. Being your own boss requires self-discipline and will-power, because there's no boss around to provide them for you.

Poor Accounting: You cannot be in control of your business if you don't know what's going on. eBay is very much a numbers game: you're constantly tweaking your offerings and recording the results – right down to 0.1¢. With bad numbers, or no numbers, you're flying

blind, and it happens all the time.

There are eBay spreadsheets that are enormously helpful. But they're only helpful if you fill them in religiously and act on the basis of what they tell you. To get an idea of how much help is available for you, consider using an eBay spreadsheet, which, for $49.95, automatically fills in:

- Your eBay Item Number
- Listing Title
- Selling Price
- Sales Tax
- Customer's Name and ID
- Customer's e-mail address
- Insertion Fees
- Final Value Fee
- Store Referral Credits
- Paypal Fee
- Payment Method
- Shipping and Handling Charged
- Paypal Shipping Information: Shipping Method Used
- Tracking Information

So there's really no need to worry about the details or entering typos. With the right setup the details will be handled for you and typos eliminated. There's no excuse...

Lack of Competitive Advantage: You may have chosen a niche that is already crowded with established products at prices that are too competitive. When you see this – and you definitely will – move on without a backward glance. It's part of the process.

Raising Your Game

Once you've found something that sells you're on your way to becoming an eBay Power seller, and then a Top-Rated Seller. Below is a brief description.

PowerSeller and Top-rated Seller

Achieving and maintaining PowerSeller and Top-rated seller status requires a proven track record of both quality and quantity. Becoming a Bronze PowerSeller is the first step. Higher sales volume will result in a higher PowerSeller tier, while higher quality will result in Top-rated seller status. PowerSeller status is required to become a Top-rated seller. A seller can track their progress toward PowerSeller requirements and Top-rated seller status through their Seller Dashboard. PowerSeller program eligibility is reviewed every month. Sellers not meeting the eligibility requirements may lose their PowerSeller status. Below are the requirements to be a PowerSeller, as well as the additional requirements for Top-rated seller status.

The requirements for and benefits of Top-rated seller status are changing, so follow the links to keep up. The minimum requirements to become and maintain PowerSeller status are:

- 90 days on site
- Account is in good standing (not past due)
- Feedback and detailed seller ratings (DSRs) requirements (details below)
- Sales volume requirements - minimum and by PowerSeller tier.

The Power Seller status gives you a number of benefits, the biggest of which is participation in Thailand Post Office's eBay Power Seller

Program which gives you

- ⅄ a 15% discount on shipping,
- ⅄ online registration of packages,
- ⅄ home pickup of your shipments,
- ⅄ door-to-door tracking and delivery confirmation of delivery for free.

That's something to shoot for, and there's help available to get you to your goal fast.

Packaging and Shipping from Thailand

Clothing and non-breakable items can be shipped in white plastic shipping envelopes. They're convenient, lighter, and cheaper than boxes. For non-clothing items, trial and error will determine what's best for you. The good news is that packaging supplies are cheap in Thailand.

Invest in a small label printer. These are thermal printers that spit out handsome adhesive labels in seconds. Thermally-printed labels won't smear, or smudge in the rain. You can add your own logo to the label which creates a good impression even before your customer opens the package.

What shipper should you use? You can experiment with UPS, DHL, and Fedex, all of which are here, but you will probably come back to the Thailand Post Office, especially once you become a Power Seller and are eligible for Track & Trace. They are convenient and cheap and often beat the private companies in delivery time.

Should you register your items? No. Unless they are unusually valuable, or your customer requests it (you can make it an extra-cost option) it's statistically not worth it. You'll typically end up paying more in registration and insurance charges than you'll save from just re-sending the occasional piece. In any case, Track & Trace does almost the same job.

This is your chance to build a brand (one which you might sell to another expat when you want to cash out and take your second retirement!) so tag every item with your brand name and website address. Design your own labels (incredibly cheap here) and apply them to everything you ship. You can get those made to order in Pratunam, the fashion suburb of Bangkok, among other places.

Outsourcing

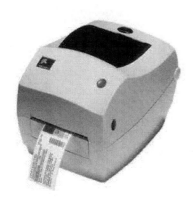

As your customer base grows the complexity of your business grows too. It's great to have hundreds of customers who tell their friends about your "wonderful little business in Thailand run by some

retirees", and for those friends to email you and ask if you still stock the same Thai school uniforms you sold a year ago? Or if they can still return the yoga pants even though it's been 6 months since they bought them? And so on. But it can distract you from your main purpose in life: having fun and selling stuff.

A friend of mine who has a thriving business selling Thai XX-size women's clothing on the Internet was always juggling about 30 different garment lines, refunds, taxes, and invoices. A year ago, on the Internet he found a woman who is confined to home and receiving disability payments. She offered to take over the entire administration of his business for $5/hour, and did a wonderful job of it. Since then he has been, he told me, "on permanent vacation".

So remember sites like peopleperhour.com and elance.com who have lots of people willing to do your e-chores for you for very little money. Don't trap yourself. You're surrounded by willing helpers.

Making a Profit

Here is the arithmetic of an item you just sold on eBay. This is an approximate average, of course, but it's close to reality because it's based on the results of the three most successful eBay sellers I know – and they're very successful indeed:

	US$	THAI-BAHT
Price You Sold the Item for on eBay	$40.00	1200
- What You Paid for that Item	-10	-300
- eBay and PayPal fees	-10	-300
- Unsold, returned, lost goods (10%)	-4	-120
= Profit (40%)	$16.00	320 Bt.

So your net profit is $16, – 40% of the $40 selling price of that item.

Perhaps that doesn't sound very exciting but if you sell just one item a day, seven days a week, you're making $480/month on one item! And $16, or 320 Baht, buys dinner for two at a nice Thai restaurant.

The final step up the ladder to prosperity is to assemble ten products selling at markups in this 4:1 – 8:1 range. That will take about two years of steady effort. But it's exciting. And remember, it will still allow you to take vacations any time you wish and travel to, say Myanmar (4 hours from Chiang Mai) where you could find some new items to sell and some grateful manufacturers and craftspeople, since Myanmar is just beginning to open up to the world.

That's the fun of living in a foreign country. You see opportunities everywhere.

CHAPTER 8: STARTING AN INTERNET BUSINESS IN THAILAND

Perhaps you find eBay too constricting and would like to have your own, independent Internet business. You don't need tangible products and you can do it from anywhere. There's nothing to buy or pack or ship or insure. Pure Internet businesses have their drawbacks too, as we will see. Your website can be in addition to your eBay store or it can be a completely different business altogether. Here's how to do it:.

A Website Business for $100

It's getting easier every day to set up a website. I'll describe the traditional approach first. After that I'll tell you about ways that are even easier. Then I'll tell you how to cheat on the whole process. The links take you to articles that give you the details, along with other good links. Just click on them to learn more. Here are the steps:

1. Choose a Domain Name
2. Buy a Domain Name
3. Buy Website Hosting
4. Set up Your On-Line Business Platform. As you'll learn, there are plenty of possible software 'platforms' (also called CMS, Content Management Software). Wordpress, the platform recommended here is excellent, it's free, and you can have a Wordpress business site up and running in 48 hours for $5.
5. Configure and Optimize your Business Platform: Out of the box, Wordpress lacks some of the features you'll want. You simply pick features you desire and plug them into Wordpress, which is why they're called 'plugins'. The easiest way to do this is to pay someone $5 for each plugin, and they'll install it for you. Here are the most popular ones:

   ⅄ All-in-one SEO Pack
   ⅄ Google XML Sitemaps

✞ Contact Form 7
✞ WordPress Super Cache
✞ Akismet Comment Spam Blocker

Wordpress can be overwhelming when you start because it is so rich in features but fear not, there are literally hundreds of articles and forums explaining every aspect of it, and the people at fiverr.com will install, fix, and explain them to you...for $5 each.

6. Set up your business website (thorough article and video)
7. Set up Your PayPal Account (it's free)

Now you're getting ready to launch. Read widely on the Internet and subscribe to every email newsletter that looks promising. The whole web business is mostly self-education. It takes a few concentrated hours every day, just as it does to learn tennis, bridge, or anything else.

A Single Website Business: Creating a Niche

There are 2.3 billion people using the Internet and that number is rising, and automatically creating new niches every day. Niche sites serve a limited audience but they are valuable to anyone who wants to provide products or services to that audience.

For example, imagine you like tie-dyed silk. It's a tiny niche, but Thailand is a world capital for such fabrics, so local resources from silk-worms all the way to couture designers and hand-painters are plentiful. If you wanted to have fabric dyed to your design, or cut to your pattern, you could do so with no problems.

Say there are a million people (0.00001% of the Internet) worldwide with sufficient interest in tie-dyed silk to visit a tie-dye silk website once a year.

That's 2,500 interested people every day of the year. And you don't even have to sell or ship anything. All you're selling is access to your visitors. Google will deposit the money automatically into your bank account, so you don't have to worry about accounting or collections, or returns, or...

Without much effort you can figure out that there are enough silk merchants, hobby-supply merchants, and travel sites that want to talk to your 2,500 visitors and will happily pay you 1¢ for each introduction. That doesn't sound like much, but

$$1¢ \times 2{,}500 \times 365 = \$10{,}000/\text{year}$$

$10,000/year for a site that you created in a week using free software and which you maintain in a few pleasurable hours each week, posting pictures and videos of your visit to a local merchant, factory, or tie-dye silk artist.

Now, to ice the cake, you could offer a Thailand Tie-Dye Tour for enthusiasts once a year. Time it to coincide with one of the spectacular local festivals, take your tour group out to dine at the local flower-petal restaurant (that's right, the entire meal is made from flower petals), then float them down the river on a dragon-tail boat...there's really no end to this gigantic, under-served market. And, incidentally, http://www.tiedyedthaisilk.com/ is available.

I've been turning to Ryan Mendenhall, in Glendale, California for Internet and search engine help. He's a serious techie who speaks English instead of jargon, and comes up with– and implements – great SEO and book-marketing stuff. He now tunes my website, my book blogs, and stuff like my Google+ profile and the way I appear when someone Googles my name.

Then he patiently makes all the pieces work synergistically. He bills me like a lawyer so if I only need 15 minutes of his time I only pay him $20. He's making a video of himself patiently helping me to do everything an author needs to do to market their book. Sign up for the newsletter at http://www.mendenhallcreative.com.

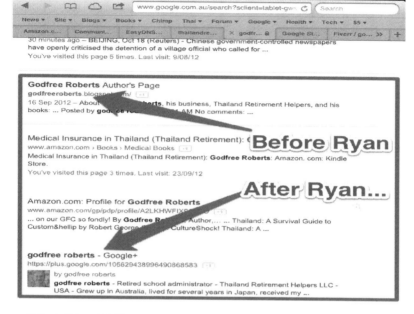

Serial Website Creation

Once you've made one website you'll realize how easy it is. The more sites you create the better and quicker you'll become at it, until you can put up a decent site in less than a day.

So why not continue creating websites? Sure, they're only 3-4 pages but they're about subjects you enjoy and are useful or amusing enough to attract a steady trickle of visitors. Don't worry about advertising. Google will handle that automatically for you and provide blog-creation software and host your site. All for free.

I created a website devoted to a pinched-nerve condition called, *Meralgia Paresthetica*, for example. Have you ever heard of it? Probably not, but tens of thousands of sufferers come to it because it's the only site devoted entirely to that condition, and it covers just about every aspect of the problem from drugs to exercises to rehabilitation. I created it using my iPad while I was lying in bed suffering from – you guessed it – meralgia paresthetica.

You'll soon figure out how to attract enough visitors to earn you $1/day from a typical site. If you plough ahead and create a site like that every week, adding some free video footage from YouTube to each one, then after two years your 100 sites will each bring in $1/day and so will be earning you a total of $100, every day, 365 days a year. That's $36,500 a year in addition to your pension.

Here are the basics of becoming a serial website creator. If you don't know anything about these things, don't worry. It's simple and it's getting simpler all the time. Google unfamiliar terms and start playing around. Take an introductory course at your local college, community center, or online by entering these search terms:

⅄ Website design,
⅄ Free Internet marketing courses,
⅄ how to use Blogger
⅄ Google's Adsense.

Then follow these easy steps:

1. Choose a subject you are passionate about and you can write about without getting bored. For example, windsurfing. Make sure there are plenty of videos about it on YouTube (there are thousands of windsurfing videos on YouTube). Just go to YouTube and enter 'wind surfing'.

2. Research popular keywords in the area. Google will give you a list of related terms – like "windsurfing equipment" or "windsurfing expeditions", etc – that people use, and tell you how many such searches there were each month. "Windsurfing" had 850,000 searches last month, for example. ("Thailand Retirement" had only 8,500).

3. Buy a Domain Name. You can own a domain name like www.ThailandWindsurfing.com for less than $10. (That domain name was available when I wrote this book).

4. Get to know either Blogger, WordPress, or a program like xsitepro, which make website creation easy. Just thrash around and make mistakes. There's no cost and no penalties.

5. Create pages of content from your own knowledge and research, friends' stories and videos, and YouTube videos of windsurfing that are royalty-free.

6. And, of course, shoot some windsurfing videos of your own when you come to Thailand!

7.Sign up for Google's Adsense.

8. Watch your PayPal account balance slowly rise.

9. Repeat x 100.

10. Go to the beach.

In writing this I've made it look as if money just grows on website trees. In reality it takes as much persistence as any new business, and just as much frustration. But you already knew that. This is not a book about free lunches. It's about businesses that will make money while you live and relax in The Land of Smiles.

Serial Website Creation for Cheaters

Instead of creating your own website you can simply go to fiverr.com or click on this link (The man's name is Vivek, he lives in India, he creates $5 websites and he's received a 100% satisfaction rating.

Here's his complete offering: *I will create 5 page WORDPRESS business website for $5. We will make a 5 page Wordpress website with custom banners and sliders according to your business in Wordpress. I have 9 years of experience in making Wordpress sites. Please provide logo and text content for Wordpress web pages with order. This gig includes at least 2 Homepage Slider Images, use of Good Icons. I will make your Wordpress website look good by matching colors and images as per your logo colors.*

So all you have to do is come up with 100 ideas, the text, photos, videos from YouTube, and $500. Vivek will do the rest. You'll be in business in 90 days. Who said cheats never prosper?

Of course, I'm deliberately making it sound easy. It's really a lot of work, like every money-making activity on the planet.

Niche Sites: Joe and Justin's Excellent Adventure

The heroes of this tale aren't anywhere close to retirement as you can see from their picture and they chose to live in the Philippines, not Thailand.

And they were technically savvy when they started their business. Why then, are they here?

Several reasons: they were willing to tell me everything I wanted to know about niche sites whereas most people I approached clammed up. Another is that they were equally willing to tell me about the money side of it. That's very unusual. A third reason is that they were willing to answer embarrassing questions, like the last one in this interview: I saw that Google has just shot down one of their biggest money-making strategies, so I asked them about it. And finally, because what they produce is something you might consider buying: ready-made niche sites that are already making some money each month.

Justin Cooke and Joe Magnotti are a trusted source of quality content in niche marketing. They have accomplished this by giving away all of their –very useful – content for free and sharing detailed income reports, all the while creating a profitable business selling the sites they create.

Even if you are not interested in building niche websites, AdsenseFlippers offers great insights into keyword research, search engine optimization, structured business processes and outsourcing – skills critical to any blogger or online business. Justin and Joe offer a fantastic introduction into niche site creation and life in the Philippines in this interview. Be sure to go to their site to download the free niche site ebook and subscribe to their podcast. You will not be disappointed.

I asked John Bardos, intrepid founder of jetsetcitizen.com, to ask Joe and Justin all the right questions. Read and learn...

John Bardos, *JetSetCitizen*: How many times have you heard that a "blog is not a business?"

Justin: Most bloggers seem to start a site with some vague hope of monetizing in the future. A much better approach is to create a business and use the website to generate customers. A blog is a fantastic way to generate awareness, drive targeted search engine optimized traffic and build trust with your audience. There is no better example of blogging to grow a business than AdsenseFlippers.com.

John: Why did you choose to locate in the Philippines?

Justin: We'd both previously worked for a local search marketing company based in Southern California. We'd spent quite a bit of time building our own outsourcing company to offer services and, when the time came, Joe and I both left our positions at that company to be vendors, outsourcing ourselves! Joe left around August 2009 and I joined him in the Philippines in January 2010. From there, we began working on our outsourcing company. We ended up losing that major client by the end of 2010, which forced us to scramble to find a way to replace that income so that we could keep our well-trained and loyal employees. Which is how we came to start AdSenseFlippers.

I'd like to say we chose Davao City, Philippines because of it's "typhoon free" status, their "ahead of the curve" position in the outsourcing industry, etc. I'd like to say that. The less interesting truth is that we'd worked with someone in Davao City with our previous Real Estate business and had an "in" that was helpful in setting our company up.

While Davao has a population of roughly 1.5M people, it still feels a bit sleepy compared to Manila or Cebu. The infrastructure isn't as strong as the two other major cities and we tend to have more power outages than they do, but the costs are significantly less as well. The average agent is on approximately 50% of the salary of the same agent in Manila, and 75% of the salary of an equivalent agent in Cebu.

John: What is your cost of living there?

Justin: If you plan to buy "international goods" (laptops, cell phones, etc.) you can expect to pay similar prices - more even and it's often for an older model.

The real benefits start kicking in when you take advantage of anything service related. A 1.5 hour massage will cost you $8 in a nice spa and $15 at the nicest place in town. Want a live-in maid? You're looking at anywhere from $15 – $30 per week. (We have two that we call "house managers" that are at the upper end of the spectrum. They're way more than just maids as they take care of everything).

You start to think about things a little differently when everything is taken care of for you. We don't do any food shopping, cooking, laundry, payment of bills, cleaning…nothing…everything's taken care of. It saves us a ton of time and lets us focus on our business and our lives. It's not something we talk much about on our blog because of our focus, but it really is pretty fascinating…I don't know how I could go back to "normal" living after this, honestly.

All of our bills are paid through the business (including "house" bills) and so the money we pay ourselves personally is truly ours. We rent a 2-story, 3-bedroom townhouse in one of the nicer subdivisions in Davao and it costs us approximately $600/month. The house is running around 20 hours a day though, with employees and friends in and out all of the time…so our "extra" bills can be quite expensive. All-in, our costs are around $3,000/month to maintain our place including rent, electricity, food, maids, all bills, etc.

With everything taken care of by the business, we only personally spend around $1,500 – $3,000 per month each, depending on whether we're taking trips more, going out more, etc. We're far from minimalists though, and like to go to the best restaurants in town, take out groups of people, etc. You can live on $1,500/month reasonably and $3,500-$4,000/month comfortably in the Philippines.

John: Tell us about AdsenseFlippers

Justin: We started AdSenseFlippers at the end of 2010. Our outsourcing company was in a rough spot, recently losing a major customer. Our thought was that we'd try out several different projects and see if we could at least cover the salaries of our agents until we could get them placed with new clients. We tried some work on Mechanical Turk and a couple other projects that didn't work out.

We came across a project that seemed to fit our skill sets quite well that involved manual creation of niche websites monetized with AdSense. Our outsourcing company specialized in breaking down complicated work processes into smaller bits, building systems that improved efficiency, and then scaling…so this seemed like a natural fit if we could make it work. It didn't at first. We spent close to $2,000 not even including our time and we only made around $33 that first month…ouch!

A few months later we had spent around $10K on the project when we finally started to turn the corner and make some money. We realized that by selling some of our niche sites off we were able to maximize cash flow and scale the process much quicker than we would have been able to otherwise.

We started our blog in May 2011, and by the end of 2011 we were bringing in quite a bit of money each month. We had a monster month in January 2012 ($45K) where we sold a bunch of sites, but our average for the last 6-8 months is in the $16K – $18K per month range. We give monthly income reports and updates to inspire others and to hold ourselves accountable.

John: What is your rationale for giving away so much free content?

Justin: This way of doing business definitely did not come naturally to us. Previously, we believed that if you have a profitable process you keep it to yourself and maximize the value as long as you possibly can. We joke this is the "old school" way of doing business…a path we were previously committed to. I'd read Chris Anderson's book *"Free: The Future Of A Radical Price"* and really liked the disruptive nature of free in industries that typically charge but, honestly, we were a little chicken-shit to apply it to our "real" business.

We viewed AdSenseFlippers as a side project, even long after it was showing some legs and turning a profit. Because this was a new venture for us, we felt much more confident in applying methods that we thought might help shake up the IM industry. Before getting involved in the IM (internet marketing) industry I have to admit we looked at it with distrust and (in Joe's case) a bit of disdain as well. We thought much of it was snake oil and weren't sure we wanted to get involved in that. Ultimately, there are plenty of charlatans in IM, but we've come across quite a few people that are not, and I think that has much to do with the fact that like attracts like, possibly?

This new model has completely changed the way we view business. Giving away our entire process step-by-step has built us authority in the niche, by showing we know what we're talking about. It's even brought us quite a few potential customers, which has given us the "wonderful problem" of having more buyers than niche sites to sell. Ultimately, it's the connections we've been able to make and the doors that have been opened that, I think, will provide us the most value.

Since starting AdSenseFlippers we've had people stopping by Davao regularly to meet us, we've met up with some amazing entrepreneurs in Puerto Galera and Bali, Indonesia, and I've met (and since had the opportunity to work with) a true business hero of mine over the last year. None of that would have happened, I think, without our first step forward with a new mindset.

John: What is a niche site?

Justin: A niche site for us is typically an information site around a few very specific keyword phrases. We first perform keyword research to find a phrase that gets enough searches each month, has marketability, and (based on our criteria) will be reasonably easy for us to rank with our process. Once we find that keyword phrase, we purchase the exact match domain and set up hosting for the site. We then put up a 500-600 word article with images that targets the specific keyword we're targeting and use that as the homepage. We then target 4 related keywords with similar search volumes and build additional pages on the site, including a Contact Us, About Us, and Privacy Policy page. Here's a quick breakdown:

- Keyword Research: $2
- Domain: $8

- Site Setup: $2
- Site Content: $19 ($5 for primary, $10 for 4 pieces of secondary content, $4.00 for time)
- Various Admin/Tracking: $5
- Link-building: $5 – $20

We've varied our link building costs over time. Currently, we're spending next to nothing, but that will be changing in the very near future as we're doing an ROI test on link building.

It's hard to put an exact time on the process as we have it fragmented out to so many different agents, but the cost of creating the site is around $30-$35 each including the domain, but without link-building. We've varied our link-building process dramatically and at different costs, but the sites ends up costing somewhere between $40-$55 each all-in. We're currently at the lower end of the spectrum because we're not doing much for link-building. That will change again over the next month or two.

The exact steps and timeline are pretty involved and more than I can cover in this answer. We lay out everything in our guide, "Building A Niche Site Empire" and I encourage you to check it out if you're interested. (We've also recently published on the Kindle! It's not free and costs $0.99…but we wanted to go "high tech" for this one, heh! heh! You can check it out here.)

John: How much does a typical 5 page niche site earn?

Justin: It normally takes 3-5 months for a site to reach its earning potential. We used to track this very specifically and found that our average site would earn $9 – $12 per month. (This can be a bit misleading though, as very few are actually in that range. 30% of our sites were bringing in 70% of the revenue, making a pretty clear delineation between those that are doing well and those that are not) We've since noticed that our sites have dropped a bit across the board, earning somewhere between $7 – $9 per month.

Over time, we've ended up selling off most of our sites that are earning over $10/month and have been with us 6 months or more, so we're left with a ton of sites that are on the very low end. If they're earning somewhere between $1-$5 per month, we'll typically package them in with other better earning sites and sell them off. If they're less than the $1.00 per month, they'd be considered a dud.

John: What percentage of your sites fail to rank and don't make money?

Justin: It used to be that around 20% of our sites wouldn't earn much at all, but that's since climbed to 25-40%. We've looked pretty hard at why some sites would make it and others wouldn't, hoping we could improve our keyword research process, but none of that research led to anything actionable, unfortunately. We simply view our failure rate as a cost of doing business at this point, although we're open to exploring it again in the future to see if we can improve our success rate.

It's strange, sometimes the sites we build don't end up ranking well at all on Google for their primary keyword, but end up picking up quite a bit of traffic from other secondary keywords we were, or even weren't targeting. Sometimes those sites end up ranking extremely well on Bing or Yahoo, helping them to earn a bit each month as well.

John: Why are niche sites a good way to make money online?

Justin: I think niche sites are a great way to get started, but I hesitate to say it's an easy way to make money. Just because we were successful at it doesn't mean that everyone else will be as well. It could be our experience with outsourcing and building processes, our enthusiasm and approach to free information, or just dumb luck!

That being said, I think building niche sites is probably the BEST way to get started. You learn the fundamentals (Keyword research, WordPress setup/hosting, content creation, link building, etc.) in a relatively low-risk, low-reward environment. Someone looking to break into IM can build a few niche sites, make mistakes, correct those, see results, etc...all in a relatively short period of time. (4-6 months) Using our methods can help others get started until they find the right fit in IM that suits their interests and skill sets. An even more robust way to "try out" making money online would be to check out Ed Dale's free *"30 Day Challenge"* from what I hear, although I haven't been through the entire course myself.

John: Are they really passive once they have search engine ranking?

Justin: Yes and No. They're passive in that they continue to earn, but the amounts have fluctuated over time. We've had sites decline month after month for 3-4 months and then have their page views and earnings pop right back up again. We've had other sites that were steady as can be and others that declined to a fraction of what they were initially earning. My guess is that there is some sort of shelf-life overall (2-4 years?) if no additional work is put into the sites. We've talked to others that have been at this much longer than we have that have sites that have been earning 3-5 years and going strong, but we're still a bit new at this and it doesn't take into account the others whose sites are not earning that long.

John: If niche sites make money, why do you sell your sites?

Justin: This was a question that Joe and I ended up arguing over early on. I wanted to put more money into the process and double-down on site creation for our long-term benefit. Joe wanted to slowly grow the business by only expanding with the passive income. We finally came to an agreement that by selling earning sites, we'd self-fund the cash flow to continue to build more so that we could get to a level of site creation that made sense. Otherwise, it would have taken us much longer to build out the process and earn a decent amount of money from the project.

We came up against this question again about 7-8 months into the project. Ultimately, our decision was based on the multiple we were getting (20-25X monthly revenue) and the fact that we had plenty of experience building small, earning niche sites, but virtually no experience building those sites out to be even larger earners. Rather than taking the investment risk and time involved in building them out we thought it would be better to focus on what we're good at, building them from scratch and getting them started so that others could take them over.

In July 2012, we'll have been at this for around 20 months. We've done the math and realized that we'd eventually come across a turning point, a point at which holding on to the sites would have been more profitable and we're getting pretty close to that now. We originally hired an intern to help us test through the process of expanding some of our niche sites, but his programming and design skills came into play and we needed him for higher priority projects. Throughout the end of this year our plan is to see if we're able to expand our niche sites and improve their earnings. We currently have a sales cycle of around 6 months on average, but I'm guessing this new process would expand that to 12-15 months if we end up selling them at all.

John: What are some of the risks of starting a business focused on building niche sites?

Justin: It's completely risk free! I'm kidding of course, there are quite a few risks to be aware of and try to mitigate as best you can. I'll give examples of some of the major risks that come to mind in the order of importance to us:

Process Doesn't Work – For whatever reason, you end up spending quite a bit of time, effort, and energy and you just can't make it profitable.

Quitting Before The Turning Point – We figured we would give it 6 months from the start, but the first two months were really depressing. Lots of work and expenses with very little return. If we would have backed out then that really would have been a waste.

Loss of ROI – At the level we're creating sites, a quick hit (AdSense account disabled, all sites deindexed, etc.) would be preferable to a slowly degraded ROI over time. This would be pretty painful in that it would be harder to catch, and ultimately cost us quite a bit of money as we went deeper into the hole.

Deindexed Sites – This is when Google removes your sites from the index, making them virtually impossible to find on Google. We've had a few sites deindexed here and there, but having this happen across the board would be quite painful.

AdSense Account Disabled – Quite a few people have dealt with this recently. You keep the sites and traffic, but end up taking a hit as other similar monetization methods aren't nearly as effective. We've written a post about AdSense alternatives and our disaster plan were this to happen to us.

I'm sure there are others, but that covers most of them - quite a few eh? I'll be honest and tell you that we try to not spend too much time thinking about them. We track everything really well, have contingency plans in place, etc. We rely on that planning so that we don't spend all of our time worrying about what "might" happen.

John: Several high profile niche marketers have been de-indexed or banned by Google recently, what are you doing to avoid this?

Justin: We've been involved in several different businesses together across multiple industries and realize the simple act of going into business for yourself is risky. What if your supplier raises the price, cutting out your margins? What if a competitor builds a better mousetrap and undercuts your pricing and value significantly? What if a competitor steals your best salesperson and your clients? TONS of risk…

An overwhelming majority of the time those who have had their AdSense accounts banned were:

1. Previously banned and tried to set up a new account
2. Using sketchy sources of non-targeted traffic to get people to their site.
3. Clicking (or encouraging others to click through friends, bots, etc.) on their own ads

I know a few of the niche marketers you're mentioning and we're pretty sure this wasn't the case with them, but it's important to keep the above in mind when it comes to banned AdSense accounts. Through some questioning, we've found that many fit into one of the three options listed above.

John: For a purchaser of your sites, what is a reasonable expectation of return on their investment?

Justin: Pretty close to half of our current websites sales are repeat purchases from previous customers. Some have reported back that their sites more than doubled in monthly earnings. (One in particular recouped his investment in 7-8 months) Others have found their earnings increased, similar, decreased, etc. over time. (20% up, 30% down, etc.) We'd love to take credit for the huge gains, but they often had to do with changes the client made to the sites. (Link building, added content, etc.)

We make this clear on our 'Buy Our Sites' page and in communication with customers, but I'll mention it here as well. We make no guarantees as to how a site will perform or when a customer can expect to see a return. That being said, a recouped investment within 2 years with an asset worth 50% or better of its initial value sets the bar pretty low, I think.

John: What is your long term plan for AdsenseFlippers?

Justin: At one point we'd discussed an exit strategy for AdSenseFlippers. (Ok, we were daydreaming about selling the company and fantasizing about what we'd do with the money!) Ultimately, I think the business and brand are too tied to us to sell to anyone. At this point, some of our focus has been on improving our technology and using our assets and data to build infrastructure and tools for our business. Selling off pieces of our business that are related to our brand but not dependent on it seems to be a reasonable path to take.

The EMD update definitely had an impact, but doesn't change our overall goals. Here's the answer to the question:

John: How is your business model going to change with the latest Google changes to exact match domains?

The EMD update rolled out by Google in late September, 2012 had a largely negative impact on our sites. We're still reviewing and analyzing the data from sites that were penalized and those that were not to determine some of the tactics that we'll have to change going forward. We've already noticed a few trends that seemed to be prevalent on negatively effected sites and not others, so we'll be adjusting our process to improve our older sites and upgrade the process as we continue to build more every week.

While this will change some of the tactics used, we believe strongly in the overall strategy. Creating useful and valuable content for users through targeted niche content that's monetized with advertising is the best way to build an online empire. It's important to keep your business process fluid and malleable, so that you can adjust to changes in niche markets and with search engines. This isn't our first setback (and not likely to be our last) so we've put provisions and plans in place that should allow us to bounce back.

John: How can people get in touch with you?

Justin: If you'd like to get in touch with us you can check out our blog at www.AdSenseFlippers.com, visit our Facebook page, check out our podcast on iTunes, or give us a shout on Twitter!

Affiliate Marketing

Website affiliate marketing is an interesting niche and, as a Thailand resident, you'll be in a position to take advantage of it if you find the notion appealing.

The idea is that you create an e-report or e-booklet on a topic that interests you and that would be of interest to others like say, Windsurfing in Thailand. You then list it on an affiliate site. Here's how expert affiliate marketer Darren Rowse describes it:

Perhaps the simplest way to explain affiliate marketing is that it is a way of making money online whereby you as a publisher are rewarded for helping a business by promoting their product, service or site.

There are a number of forms of these types of promotions, but in most cases they involve you as a publisher earning a commission when someone follows a link on your blog to another site, where they then buy something.

Other variations on this are where you earn an amount for referring a visitor who takes some kind of action – for example when they sign up for something and give an email address, where they complete a survey, where they leave a name and address, etc.

Commissions are often a percentage of a sale but can also be a fixed amount per conversion. Conversions are generally tracked when the publisher, you, uses a link with a code only being used by you embedded into it that enables the advertiser to track where conversions come from (usually by cookies). Other times an advertiser might give a publisher a 'coupon code' for their readers to use that helps to track conversions.

For example: when I recently released my *'31 Days to Build a Better Blog Workbook'* I also give people an opportunity to promote the workbook with an affiliate program whereby they could earn a 40% commission for each sale. When you sign up to become an affiliate you are given a special code unique to you, which enables you to promote the workbook and make $7.98 per sale. The top affiliates earned over $2000 in the first few weeks after launch through these commissions.

So, you could create an e-Booklet called Windsurfing in Thailand: Where to Go; What to Pay; Where to Stay; Who to Meet; Where to Drink, and sell it on your website for 99¢. That's great value. Even I'd pay 99¢ for just the 'where to stay' information, and I'm not a windsurfer! Thousands of people will pay for your creation. Which means that advertisers will be attracted to your site, which means...

Write, Dammit! Write! The World of Online Writing

If you can't string two sentences together or find writing a chore then skip this section. There are plenty of other opportunities.

But if you can put together a couple of hundred semi-coherent words while sitting by the river, waited on hand and foot by lovely Thai girls, then this could be exactly what you're looking for.

You see, just as TV has an insatiable hunger for creative content so does the Internet. People expect Internet content to be current and relevant. And that's where writers come in.

I personally know a guy here in Chiang Mai who started off writing for money, then began hiring people to do it for him then, after 3 years, sold half his business for $500,000. He's still at it and his income is still increasing. I've written three ebooks and I can promise you that there's plenty of room for more. Plenty.

Here's an excellent blog post that not only tells you how to make money writing while you're living in Thailand, but shows you how the money part works and how much the writer herself makes.

CHAPTER 9: A HOME-BASED BUSINESS IN THAILAND

Freelancing

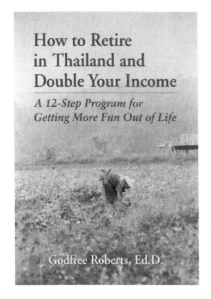

There are many websites that bring freelancers together with potential customers. Here are four very successful ones. Visit each of them. Look at the wild variety of things that freelancers are offering. Daniel Green is offering to "make a 30-second video of myself dancing in spandex with a happy-birthday message". Another freelancer *"will show you how to prepare for the toughest job interviews"*.

Type in some job descriptions for things you could do. Here are two examples of work their freelancers did for me, my book covers, along with what I paid.

I paid a freelance artist $150 to design the first cover (right) for my book, *How to Retire in Thailand and Double Your Income*, but friends said that it was too laid-back and suggested I try a more dynamic design.

I'd already spent $150 on the original design and couldn't afford to do it again so I contacted *fiverr.com*, and found a listing that said, "Design a professional cover for your eBooks". I sent $5 via PayPal along with my original picture and, 48 hours later, the new design (below) came back. I haven't used the new version yet, but I plan to test it soon.

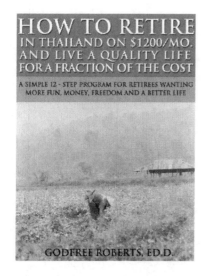

I was so pleased with the price that I sent off my back cover material and another $5 and sure enough, 2 days later the result, below, was in my inbox.

Here are some freelance agencies to get you started. I've used the first three of them and been happy with the results:

fiverr.com,
elance.com
PeoplePerHour.com
FreelanceCareers.com

The morals of this story are:

1. You can make $5 (and there are $10 and $25 sites) very quickly for almost anything.

2. If you have a skill and want to make some quick bucks, try advertising it on one of these sites.

3. If you need a service, check these sites first. They can literally save you thousands.

Indeed, looking on the Internet for inexpensive services is the prudent first step.

peopleperhour.com
This site brokers professional services like programming and website creation. I found a team of young programmers willing to create my website, *ThailandRetirementHelpers.com*, for $800. It was a lot of work for them and for me, but the result was an excellent first effort and got me started. Take a look at it to see what you can get for $800.

Freelance Careers
If you can write, Freelancer Careers usually have 400-500 freelance

writing jobs available for you to bid on. The jobs range from writing website pages and ad copy to Ph.D. dissertations.

elance.com

Elance is another freelance site that's well worth investigating. Though I've never used it, it has a very good reputation with both buyers and sellers, it's the top freelance site in the world and has more than 650,000 unique monthly visitors to the site. That's a lot of people who want work done for them. Here's some general advice about successful freelancing:

Test your service first by advertising the service you want to provide and seeing what bids come in. You need to sign up for at least 3 months and spend a few hours each day on your freelance site just to get to know how it works. On *elance.com*, for example, that 3 months will cost you $150. It allows you to set your own price, choose your own gig, and market yourself to an international audience. There are 3 ways you can work on *elance.com*:

a.) Put up samples of your work with your profile, and attach your phone number. Let people call and talk to you. That's much more comforting for them. Give out your Skype address to make it free, the video aspect adds further assurance.

b.) If your service lends itself to it, develop some pre-priced 'packaged' services that people can click on and 'Buy Now'.

c.) Bid on projects. elance.com will automatically send you every request for services that fit your expertise. Just submit your bid and sit back.

Here are the major steps to a successful bid:

1. Find (or create) your niche and bid exclusively in it. It's important to have a niche since you're competing with hundreds of people like yourself and you want to get really, really good. Besides, the market is the entire globe, so even an obscure niche can serve a lot of people.

2. Match Your Skills to the Project. Do you really have the

experience, expertise, and passion to carry the job through to a successful conclusion?

3. Set up Alerts for New Projects in Your Niche. elance.com is good about this: they'll send you notices by email, Twitter, RSS - everything but carrier pigeon.

4. Investigate the Buyer. Find out the buyer's name; look up the buyer's website, analyze the buyer's past feedback, Google the buyer's name to pick up any stray information. You're about to commit a chunk of your life to this person. It's just sound business sense to make sure that you're not dealing with a jerk.

5. Follow up: A good follow-up can double your success rate. Try starting something like this, "Dear _____, I've been giving some more thought to your job and a idea occurred to me. Why don't we simply..."

6. Write the bid using these guidelines:

Personalize it
Match the tone of your bid to the person or the project or both
Start with your strongest, most unique qualification
Make it easy for the buyer to scan - use boldface and bullet points
Orientate it towards the benefits you provide
Answer every question, including the un-asked ones
Re-state your main points
Discuss the samples you've attached
Proofread it carefully. Typos and misspellings can doom a proposal
Sign it and attach your links, then remember to test your links before hitting 'send'

CHAPTER 10: EXPORTING

Almost any product with a high labor content will be cheap in Thailand because labor here is much cheaper than in the West. So exporting makes a lot of sense. There are several ways to set up an export business:

One: Buy a few dozen items wholesale here and ship them to your friend/partner at home for resale or distribution.

Two: Buy wholesale here then take them back with you to sell at home.

Three: Buy wholesale here then sell individually on the Internet. I describe this process in detail in the next section because I think you'll find it the most attractive. You can enjoy a Thai lifestyle while making about the same net profit as the other two.

Sourcing Products in Thailand

If you're as lazy as I am just stroll down the aisles of a local, Thai-owned, upscale supermarket. You could literally spend all day there, half the time trying to figure out what some of the items are.

That's the beauty of exporting Thai products: they're new to our home market. And novelty sells. Novel products are everywhere in Thailand and they're cheap, just waiting for someone with imagination and flair to present them to consumers back home.

Each year Chiang Mai, where we host our workshops, holds an

enormous exhibition of locally made wares, from fruit wines to labeling machines. I've seen some wonderful stuff there that would sell well anywhere. The stall-holders are dying to meet someone who knows how to expose their wares to a wider market.

Bangkok Trade Fairs

January

Thailand Health and Beauty Show (Thai HBS 2011)
25-27 January 2012 (10:00 – 18:00 hrs.)
Website: www.hbsfair.com

March

Thailand International Furniture Fair (TIFF 2012)
14-16 March 2012 (10:00 – 18:00 hrs.)
Website: www.thailandfurniturefair.com

Thailand International Education Expo (TIEE 2011)
30 March – 1 April 2012
Website: www.thailandeducationfair.com

April

Bangkok International Gift Fair and International Housewares Fair
17-20 April 2012 (10:00 – 18:00 hrs.)
Website: www.bigandbih.com

Thailand Auto Parts & Accessories Fair (TAPA 2012)
26-28 April 2012 (10:00 – 18:00 hrs.)
Website: www.thailandautopartsfair.com

May

World of Food Asia 2012 (THAIFEX 2012)
23-25 May 2012 (10:00 – 18:00 hrs.)
Website: www.thailandfoodfair.com

June

Bangkok Fashion Fair and Bangkok Leather Fair (BIFF & BIL 2012)
27-29 June 2012 (10:00 – 18:00 hrs.)

Website: www.biffandbil.com

August
Made in Thailand (MIT 2012)
15 – 17 Aug 2012 (10:00 – 18:00 hrs.)
Website: www.madeinthailandfair.com

September
Bangkok Gems & Jewelry Fair (GEMS 2012)
Website: www.bangkokgemsfair.com

October
Bangkok International Gift Fair, Bangkok International Housewares Fair
(16-19 October 2012 (10:00 – 18:00 hrs.)
Website: www.bigandbih.com

November
Thailand Health and Beauty Show (Thai HBS 2012)
7-9 November 2012 (10:00 – 18:00 hrs.)
Website: www.hbsfair.com

Finding a Manufacturer

It's sometimes difficult to track down the manufacturer of a product you admire. Retailers don't want to be bypassed and many products do not have the manufacturer's name on them.

In that case you can approach the local trade council. In Thailand there are national, provincial, regional, and city trade councils dedicated to connecting overseas buyers with local manufacturers. If you ask nicely they'll do your sleuthing for you.

If it's an important lead and you're not making progress you can offer a reward of 5,000 – 10,000 Baht ($170-$300) to the official who makes the connection for you. Speak to a Thai friend before you do so, to make sure that your offer will be welcomed. Offering money to public officials is a time-honored custom here and greatly appreciated because government salaries are low.

Though it may appear to you that she is 'just doing her job', offering a gift to an official is regarded as good manners. And, of course, when you next need a favor you can return to that official secure in the knowledge that you have a friend in the department.

Speaking of time-honored customs, remember to give a gift to any official who performs a real service for you. "Gifts" are formalized, packaged gift-baskets (usually wrapped in gold cellophane) that are sold in department stores and dedicated gift stores. They are graduated in price and prestige. Ask a Thai friend to advise you on the appropriate price of the gift for your intended recipient. A $10-$15 gift basket is usually adequate. It's the thought that counts.

It's customary for regular clients to give gifts at certain times of the year, and officials are thrilled to have an office crammed with gift-baskets to proudly show off to colleagues and family. Formal gifting – as contrasted to financial corruption – is part of the culture and well worth studying.

Finding and Choosing Products to Sell

Ignore mass-produced tourist junk. Look for items that are unique and that will have a far greater value in your home market than they do here.

If you see something appealing that needs to be adapted to suit your market, buy at least one of them to demonstrate that you are serious. Then approach the manufacturer (most Thai manufacturers are small and local) and explain what you want. You'll find them eager, flexible, and intelligent partners.

If your request involves considerable work for them, agree on a price and quantity and give them a deposit. Of course you'll want to see a prototype before production begins.

Thai craftsmanship is of a high order and if you can find something that you are genuinely enthusiastic about then, with persistence and ingenuity, you can start making money.

You can do your market testing very cheaply online while you are in Thailand, then take the more successful lines back home (or send them in bulk to your home-based partner) to make bigger money.

If you are creative, energetic, and enthusiastic about what you do then you can start with little money and do very well indeed. There is no upper limit to this. As you get deeper into the process you will see other opportunities. Who knows, you might eventually find yourself exporting container loads of rice-cookers or dairy machinery.

Or you might find yourself at the beach, letting a few products sell themselves. It's your choice.

Here's a typical local success story. I told it in my first book, How to Retire in Thailand and Double Your Income. It bears repeating:

An Exporting Story

One of our first workshop attendees is a woman who now makes a comfortable income selling Thai children's clothes, which are stylish, sturdy, and cheap. We didn't teach her how to do this - we taught her how to live comfortably here on her $1330/month pension.

She sells to American parents and reaches new customers via eBay. On her own website she caters to her repeat customers. Children's clothes don't last long so her repeat business is strong.

She loves doing it, and does it from home. She didn't have to incorporate here or in the US, she's not breaking any Thai laws because she is not 'working' here, and she's selling Thai goods abroad, which the Government encourages.

Her eBay customers and her own website customers pay her via PayPal, and she also uses PayPal to pay her vendors. Her profits stay in her US bank account until she wants to transfer them here or simply use her US ATM card.

I asked her how long it took her before her business broke even? And how much did she lose before she broke even? Her response:

13 months and $2,300 – which means she lost about $200/month for over a year.

Most of that time she was testing. She sold clothes for less than they cost, gave free shipping, and made every mistake in the book. But she hung in there and now she's left things in the capable hands of a Thai employee while she goes back to Michigan to spend the summer months with her family.

She'd already learned at our workshop how to live comfortably on her $1350/month pension, so she could afford to sell her products with a relatively small markup because, as she told me, "It was just icing on the cake. Imagine what it was like for me to double my income. I was over the moon!" She's one happy lady.

Being a Manufacturer

Thailand is full of resources and talent that the outside world knows nothing about. For example, it grows dozens of medicinal plants that are effective in treating a variety of human ailments and can be cheaply purchased, in bulk, at country farmers' markets.
It is home to skilled woodcarvers and silversmiths. It grows foods that you've never heard of. In other words, it is virgin territory for entrepreneurs.

Yet Another Business Idea

I know a Thai doctor of herbal medicine who speaks excellent English and would gladly help you design, say, a herbal soap or a cold remedy using local herbs.

Then it's just a matter of experimenting in your kitchen, packaging the result, and testing it on eBay. And www.thailandherbalcosmetics.com was available when I wrote this, so it looks as though nobody's doing it.

CHAPTER 11: REAL-WORLD JOBS

Before we start talking about real-world businesses in Thailand it's important to talk about the people you'll be doing business with. If you were thinking of doing business in England, I might say a few words about warm beer and that would be enough. If it was Germany, there are some significant discussions to have about language, manners, customs, dress, etc. But Thai culture is nothing like our Western culture. So please read the introductory section of this book carefully. You may not understand Thai culture by the time you're finished, but at least you'll know that you don't understand it – and that alone can save you a lot of time, money and heartache.

There are opportunities here for products and services from your home country, and there are opportunities here for better-run businesses of every kind. Here are just some of them:

Service Broker

If you have experience in any service industry, consider putting it to work in Thailand. Printing is an example of a service (greeting cards, prints/posters, wrapping paper) are much cheaper in Thailand than the West. So long as you are not exporting copyrighted designs there could be a market for this and many similar services which a clever, industrious, and low-paid labor force can provide.

VideoBlogger

If video is your thing you're in luck. Every website on earth, including

hundreds of blogs, is now converting to using video and good footage is in demand on every subject imaginable. You could easily email every Thailand (beach-, jungle- river, wildlife)-related website on earth and offer them 30-60second clips on their topic for the $30 that is the average price per clip for the non-exclusive use of, say 2 minutes of your video footage which, of course, you can re-sell as often as you wish. And, furthermore, there is no stock footage of Chiang Mai, the ancient cultural capital of Thailand. So there's no shortage of opportunity.

Your first thought though, should go to your own websites and blogs, where attractive and interesting footage will bring you the highest earnings.

Bringing People to Thailand

Attracting people to Thailand can be very lucrative and surprisingly easy because everyone wants to visit Thailand. Don't you? You don't have to twist anyone's arm to get them to visit Thailand.

To take one example: every year thousands of people around the world study to become teachers of English as a foreign language (TEFL), a career which once served me very well and which I discuss elsewhere in this book.

I have a friend here whose school provides TEFL instruction and certification. I have done evaluations for his student teachers and can guarantee that their courses are excellent. I wish I had taken such a course before I started teaching English in Japan.

His instructor is superb, the classroom materials are first-class, the students are very happy, and they all get jobs as soon as they graduate because the school has a good reputation.

But he doesn't know how to get the word out to potential students that:

- His month-long course is great. Intense, but really, really good

- His students love it
- They all get jobs immediately
- The course is held in Chiang Mai, the world's most beautiful city
- The course fee is half what they'd pay at home because it's Thailand
- They get free accommodation in the hotel where the course is held
- They get to practice teaching on Thai kids, so they grok the culture

He'd gladly pay someone $150 for every student they enroll in his school. I was really tempted because it's actually pretty easy, but I've got my own business to attend to. If you think you could do it, you only have to enroll 1 student each week to pick up $10,000 extra income each year. And there are hundreds of opportunities like that in Thailand today. Right now, deluxe spas and hotels need guests. The list is endless.

Your own interests, experience, and expertise are good guides here. If you see something in Thailand and think, "Gee, I'll bet Molly back home would love to come here for that", then you can assume that there are a million people in the English-speaking world who are already coming here for it.

After that it's just a matter of figuring out how to reach each of those people through one of your $5 websites and, for a modest fee, offering to plug them in when they get here. All you have to do is attract a tiny fraction of them to come and presto! You've doubled your income. (See The Art Crowd, below, for an example of people who are coming anyway but don't know how to plug into the art scene in Thailand).

Providing for People Already Coming to Thailand

Provide a service like Thailand Retirement Helpers for a niche group. After all, those of us who are seriously interested in retiring to Thailand are a tiny niche. Only 8,500 people search Google each month for that phrase. Yet it's big enough to provide a comfortable

income for me – and for others who cater to sub-niches, like rich people wanting to retire here.

In fact, there's a local guy whose business provides not only accommodation, but also live-in Thai 'wives' for bachelor retirees. Talk about one-stop shopping!

Special Care Services

Most people in the West who want to provide a nice environment for their Alzheimer's relatives find that they cannot afford the desirable facilities, and cannot bear to commit loved ones to substandard places where the patients are heavily sedated and receive unskilled care.

So several of them who know about the legendary quality of Thai nursing wrote us asking if we could help? After checking around I found several beautiful facilities with wonderful care (daily swims, 24-hour companionship, hand-holding) for a fraction of their cost back home.

There are only a few hundred such people each year for whose Alzheimer's relatives Thailand is a real alternative, but they save hundreds of thousands of dollars and enjoy real peace of mind when they place their relatives here. So they are happy to pay a fee for our investigation and for teaching them the ins and outs of living in Thailand.

The Art Crowd

There are 20 million visitors to Thailand each year. Offer to serve the otherwise unserved, or poorly served interests/needs of 1% of them, like the tie-dye crowd. If only 1% of them accept your invitation and each pays you $100, you've added $25,000 to your income. That's enough extra money for two people to go anywhere on earth and stay for 2 months every year.

Now here's an example of a possible service that would be fun:

Thailand is one of the world's art Meccas. Talented artists grow like weeds here. Sooner or later every famous artist comes to visit Thailand. And for every famous artist there are 1,000 non-famous, amateur artists and 10,000 art-lovers who come here but don't know who to talk to, or where to go, or where to stay.

Local artists, galleries, and resorts would kill to get a steady stream of qualified, art-loving potential customers and will gladly spend a day serving them tea and cookies and introducing them around. Visiting (non-famous) artists would all love to have introductions to the local scene. And not only art-lovers, but artists are major buyers of other artists' work, interestingly enough.

I personally like hanging out at one of the local galleries in the countryside just outside Chiang Mai. The location is beautiful, the gallery building is exquisite, its garden and coffee shop are drop-dead gorgeous, they have free WiFi, the owner is extremely knowledgeable about the Thai art scene and speaks excellent English. I know that they'd love to have more visitors and, especially since it is the Thai custom, would gladly pay you commissions on the artworks your clients purchase.

Your tours could take in not only contemporary artists, but museums, temples, and ethnic folk artists living in villages outside town. It's a lot of work to research all of these possibilities and weed out the mediocre ones, but once you plug into the art scene here your knowledge and your circle of contacts will grow.

Imagine getting paid for sitting in one of the world's loveliest gardens, sipping iced coffee and chatting about art - while at the same time charging your grateful clients a fee for the privilege, and receiving commissions on any art they purchase.

Just in case you think that would be expensive to set up and operate, your only investment would be $5 for your website and the rental of a deluxe, air-conditioned van. It's a 15-passenger, 3-liter Toyota turbo-diesel and costs 1,500 baht ($50) per day, including a professional driver. So you can be an art tour guide with no risk since you will only rent a van when you have confirmed visitors.

And your tour groups don't have to be art enthusiasts. They could be people interested in anything from ethnography to paragliding, depending on your own interests. Just set up your website and watch your inbox fill up. (Since the name www.thailandarttours.com is available as of this writing, I assume that nobody is doing art tours here).

Accountants, Business Professionals, Buyers, Lawyers

Multinationals doing business here are reluctant to pay $200,000 'expat packages' and send staff from home because:

They are very expensive, and the staff from home may not like living in Thailand (yes, I know).

So they try to find people who are already here and who do not need the 'expat package'.

If you have a professional background, are thinking of moving here, and want to work for a few more years, now is the time to start looking for a job in Thailand. Start by Googling 'jobs Thailand [accounting]', or whatever your specialty is. Get updated on LinkedIn and start networking. (When I Googled 'jobs Thailand accounting' just now I got 58 job openings for English-speaking accountants).

Do your due diligence on any prospective Thai employer thoroughly. Thailand is notorious for scams like boiler-room telephone solicitors and other on-the-edge businesses (it's like Florida in this respect). Tread warily when you're looking for professional employment here in the Land of Smiles.

Services Broker

Paper and printing are inexpensive here and the quality of the work is high. If you know something about this field you could arrange for design and printing of, say, 100,000 shopping bags for a retailer back home. It's pleasant work and requires very little time. There are many services in Thailand that are much cheaper than they are at home.

Actor/Model/Musician

There is interest in talented people in these careers. It's not steady, but it can be rewarding if you build your own personal value. American music is appreciated here, even American Country Music. Of course there are competitors from every corner of the globe. Filipino bands, for instance, are famously talented and will work cheaper than typical American expat musicians.

Non-Profits

Most Thais live in the countryside and once you get outside the cities you'll see that Thailand is still very much a developing nation. As a result there are opportunities here for charitable and non-profit work which is emotionally rewarding. International organizations and church missionaries need as much help as they can get. Getting started in this career often requires several years of doing volunteer work however, unless you have a particular expertise, like non-profit accounting.

Licensing Agent

As Thailand moves out of second-world status it's upping its game in almost every area. If you haven't lived in a developing country you will be surprised at how uneven standards can be. In fact sometimes there are no standards at all. I notice this everywhere.

For example, when I buy a bottle of milk manufactured locally by a Japanese company I find that the cap unscrews and snaps away from its retaining ring perfectly, every time. Similarly, the inner adhesive seal is seated perfectly on the bottle aperture un-peels easily and evenly, without tearing. Its Thai competitor's product forces me to wrestle to unscrew the cap because it's retaining ring does not grip the bottle. The inner seal tears when I try to remove it, etc. You get the picture.

Now Thailand is beginning to embrace international standards like ISO-9000, in practically everything they do. In education there are all kinds of standards for things like speaking English, and every year there are hundreds of internationally-monitored English proficiency tests administered to Thais, starting with 'hotel English' all the way up to 'Ph.D. student English' for those wanting to attend foreign universities.

If this kind of work interests you, start investigating in your own field, like nursing or engineering, to see if your background might be useful. Such work is well paid, but intermittent, which suits most retirees very well.

Foreign Business' Agent

Most manufacturers back home would love to sell their products into the Thai market of 65,000,000 people whose economy is growing at 7% annually. But they cannot afford the minimum of $200,000 a year to send someone from the USA, UK, or Australia. But you could do that job for $20,000, in your spare time.

If you have a background in their industry they might want to talk to you about being their agent in Thailand. Maybe they could provide just a car and cover your expenses and commission. You would work when it pleases you.

You're already financially independent and living in Thailand, you can afford to take the time required to develop the business relationships that are so critical to doing business here. A visiting rep has very

limited time, and a resident expat would be under unbearable pressure to produce results because he would be costing his employer $20,000/month.

What if it takes a couple of years and dozens of visits to land your first contract? You get a lesson in Thai culture and Thai language every time you make a call on the local customer. And when the contract does come through your entire financial situation changes overnight. So don't throw away your years of experience just because you're moving to Thailand. Bring it with you!

Photographer

Thailand is perhaps the most photogenic country on earth. If you can take good pictures and can identify a niche then you can syndicate your photographs world wide with a mouse-click.

Diving Instructor

If diving is your passion, then Thailand is the opportunity to both indulge it and make a living at the same time.

English-speaking diving instructors are in constant demand here because perfect English is vital in life-and-death situations. Your income will vary greatly depending on the season, from a low of 25,000 to a high of 60,000 Baht ($850-$2000) monthly.

Interested? Mermaids Scuba Diving Career Training in Thailand will not only help you get certified, they'll even handle your visa for you. Give them a call or email them, they're very responsive and good people to work with.

CHAPTER 12: BUYING OR STARTING A THAI-BASED BUSINESS

There are several factors to consider when buying or starting a business with a physical location in Thailand:

- ⚔ One: You're comfortable being an entrepreneur
- ⚔ Two: You have experience in your intended line of business
- ⚔ Three: You can speak Thai
- ⚔ Four: You have enough capital to survive two years of losses

As you will see, there are tons of business opportunities in Thailand. The economy here is growing at 7% annually and it's people's tastes and interests are broadening quickly.

Buying a Thai Business: Sixteen Factors to Consider
What should you look for when buying a business in Thailand?

1. Cost of the business: or "key money" as it is often called here. Key money will depend on the income from the business. As a starting point in your calculations figure on 3x the audited profits averaged over the last 3 years.

2. Contracts and Lawyers: A written, signed contract drawn up by your own lawyer and not the other party's lawyer. Use a foreign national working in a Thai law firm, preferably one from your native country. This is more expensive but worth every penny because they will fill you in on local business realities. They are unlikely to sell you out, as may happen if your Thai lawyer succumbs to pressure from your Thai seller. Thais are fiercely nationalistic and tend to see foreign businessmen as bigger, tougher, and wealthier than them, which justifies legal hanky-panky. I can recommend a law firm here in Chiang Mai with offices through-out Thailand with foreign partners if you need it.

3. Verified Ownership: Make sure the business really does belong to the seller. Don't buy the Brooklyn Bridge just because it's in Thailand!

4. Background: Check with the electricity, utility, and equipment leasing companies to see that the bills have been paid punctually for the past 36 months (gaps indicate cash-flow problems) and are current.

5. Leases: Some leases are year-to-year, so if you start making money next year your lease payments could increase.

6. Partners: You may need a partnership for some kinds of business. Ask your lawyer about this at your first meeting. Finding good partners is difficult anywhere.

7. Work Permits: Ask your lawyer if you need a work permit. If so, they will help you structure your business so that it is a Thai corporation that employs you.

8. Licenses: Depending upon your business you may require licenses from the government, most of which can only be held by Thai nationals. This applies to cigarette, liquor and food licenses, for example. It calls for very careful contract-writing to protect you.

9. Neighbors: Neighbors can be a wonderful help. Start by talking to them about flooding, and about power and water interruptions.

10. Employees: Employees are very inexpensive in Thailand and over-staffing is the rule. But if you are not running your business yourself you must be prepared to get ripped off.

11. Management: is the key to success in Thailand as it is anywhere. If you have a gift for managing people then you are halfway home. If you need to hire such a person you will become completely dependent on them, which makes you vulnerable.

12. Front Person: You will probably need someone with hospitality skills who speaks English and can interact on your behalf with foreigners and government departments. To find such a person is difficult, especially since you also need them to be completely honest.

13. Location: location, location is the critical factor in retailing. Good

parking lots and plentiful foot traffic are important, but prime rents for such locations can be as high as 40,000 Baht/month here in provincial Chiang Mai and higher in Bangkok.

14. Theme: Exactly what do you want to do? Do you have the capital to invest in signage, marketing and shop decor? Can you make your place a destination that people will choose because of word-of-mouth?

15. Competition: Analyze it, and as you do, remember that your competitors are locals so they have an advantage over you before you even start. What advice would you give a retired Thai who wanted to set up business in your home town?

16. Corruption: Thailand is a developing country where 'rule of law' is a novelty and something that few people trust. They prefer to rely upon relationships and gifts. It's worked for them for a thousand years. Can you make it work for you?

Yet Another Business Idea

I love traditional, south-central Thai curries, the kind made with a coconut-milk base. That's what most of us think of as 'Thai food'. I've cooked hundreds of them and eaten at dozens of Thai restaurants throughout the world.

But here in Chiang Mai you cannot find a decent Thai curry. Why? Because, until the 1930s, northern Thailand was a separate kingdom, called Lanna, with its own king and its own proud culture and cuisine. Northern Thais do not make coconut milk-based curries, do not know how to make them, and have no interest in learning. They love khao soi, a Burmese-style soup-like dish made with deep-fried crispy egg noodles, pickled cabbage, shallots, lime, ground chillies fried in oil, and meat in a curry-like sauce.

Chiang Mai receives 15 million foreign visitors a year, most of whom are expecting to eat Thai curries of the kind we are used to. But all they can find is Lanna-style khao soi.

I think a 'real' Thai restaurant, serving southern-style food would be

extremely popular and profitable in Chiang Mai. It would literally have no competition in the square mile that makes up Chiang Mai's tourist center. In that square mile, 500,000 tourists walk past your restaurant door every month, hungry from walking all day and looking for 'real' Thai food. That's 125,000 people a week, or almost 20,000 famished tourists daily who would pay twice the local rate ($2.50) for a good Thai curry and still think they're getting a bargain.

Because of relaxed regulations here, such a restaurant could be launched for $50,000. So if you're a cook, love Thai food, have $50,000, and are looking for adventure, get in touch with me and I'll take you on a tour and show you what I'm talking about. Why? Because I'm dying for a good (southern) Thai curry.

CHAPTER 13: BUSINESS AND THAI LAW

Here's a rough idea of what it costs to incorporate a serious business in Thailand. Smaller businesses can be set up for less.

Company setup, registration tax, VAT	15,000 ThB
12-month non-immigrant B visa	15,000
12-month work permit	15,000
Lawyer travel & filing time	5,000
Legal fees	50,000
Government incorporation fees	31,000
TOTAL	**81,000 ThB ($2,700)**

Thai corporate law requires a minimum of 3 directors, one of whom must be Thai, and a minimum capitalization 2 Million Baht or $70,000, which does not require that amount in cash.

If you are interested in incorporating in Thailand, contact me and I'll introduce you to a local British solicitor who handles most expats in Chiang Mai (including mine). He will explain everything in English and help you to work around obstacles.

CHAPTER 14: THE TOP FIVE THAILAND BUSINESS MISTAKES

Business is business anywhere in the world. But doing business in a different county, culture, and language adds a some considerations:

1. **Experience:** Do you have real experience in the line of business you want to start? If you want to open a bar and you've run a pub in Perth, you're halfway there. If you haven't, look out. Pubs and bars are a tough game anywhere There are 1,000 of them in Bangkok alone. And that's only the 'official' ones.

2. **Capital**: Thailand's economy is seasonal, since most visitors arrive in the Thai winter. Do you have $50,000 - $150,000 you can afford to gamble with? Can you survive the 6 low-season months for 2-3 years while you build profitability? The bills will keep coming in even though the customers won't.

3. **Effort:** Did you come to Thailand to work 7 days a week 'til 10 o'clock at night? That's what your competitors will be doing.

4. **Partners:** You may be legally required to have a Thai partner. Good partners are hard to find anywhere, let alone in a foreign country when you don't yet speak the language.

5. **Law:** It's a developing country, so the law here is still pretty shaky and biased towards locals. Corruption is still a factor.

Now, despite all of this, there are plenty of expats here who have nice, profitable, local businesses. If you attend one of our workshops you'll meet some of them, so don't despair just yet.

CHAPTER 15: GET A JOB: TEACH ENGLISH IN THAILAND

When they first come to Thailand a couple will often decide that one will get a job while the other starts a business. Once the business is profitable both can devote themselves to it full time. This approach is a balance of prudence and entrepreneurialism because it allows you to sustain the inevitable first year or two of losses and make the unavoidable mistakes without getting anxious or depressed.

In early 2012 the Government of Thailand announced an ambitious new program to promote and fund the teaching of English in schools, so you are coming at a good time. English teachers are much in demand here and English-teaching jobs are plentiful. More importantly, foreigners are welcome and visas are readily provided, whereas most employee positions are reserved for Thais.

As the country develops and becomes more integrated with the global economy, English has become a necessity for businesspeople and business graduates. And with 25 million English-speaking visitors a year, most Thais are exposed to the language very directly. All hotel workers are now required to speak some English, for example, and kids in schools understand the importance of English to their careers.

Foreign teachers' salary range from 25,000 – 50,000 ThB ($850-$1,650) per month (almost twice what local teachers get) assuming that you work full time, 9 a.m. – 3 p.m. You can double that by giving private lessons. In addition, your employer must supply you with a Thai work permit and some schools provide free housing.

Thai government regulations require that you have both a tertiary degree and a TEFL (Teacher of English as a Foreign Language) certificate. Though many schools, in their eagerness to recruit native English speakers, will overlook one of these requirements depending on your experience and personality.

You can obtain your TEFL certificate at home, but there are

excellent TEFL schools here in Thailand, which are not only much less expensive ($1500, including accommodation) but have the added advantage of allowing you to do your supervised teaching with Thai children. This is invaluable because your supervisors can explain Thai schools' cultural differences.

Having supervised TEFL students here I can tell you that the course is a lot of fun and that the kids are extremely sweet!

There are bogus TEFL schools which teach you little, don't charge much, and give you a certificate that is 'legal' but has very little to recommend it. Most Thai school administrators know about these scams and are reluctant to hire anyone who shows up with such a credential.

Real TEFL schools provide at least 80 hours of classroom instruction during which you mostly rehearse your lessons in front of your peers, plus 20 hours supervised teaching of Thai classes. The best TEFL classes I have ever seen are conducted by a chief instructor named Peter Bartolomy, in Chiang Mai. We take all our workshop participants to sit in on one of Pete's classes and they always come away inspired.
If you think that this might be an avenue for you, write me…and make sure you bring all the originals of your academic transcripts and qualifications to Thailand with you. Such documents are easy to get your hands on at home but much more difficult to obtain once you're here.

Once you get your TEFL certificate the best sources for English language teaching jobs is unitefl.com's own placement service, and www.ajarn.com. Ajarn means "teacher" in Thai, and ajarn.com will tell you everything you need to know to get started teaching in Thailand, and they have lots of job listings.

The TEFL certificate has the added advantage of being accepted in 100 countries, so you could teach for a year in China, for example, where the demand for English language teachers is insatiable.

One of the biggest benefits of landing a job at a Government school is becoming eligible for Thai Social Security Medical Insurance. If you can qualify for this, all you have to do it pay a few hundred dollars a year and you have insurance for life. This is a very big deal.

The Academic Year

Thailand's academic year is the same length as ours: 40 weeks. It's divided into two 20-week terms. Most schools have a 3-week break in October and a 9-week break around Songkran (the four day, nationwide water fight) in April. If the school is Christian, they'll generally take a week off the October holiday and have a short Christmas/New Year break. In addition to the school holidays there are the Thai public holidays:

- New Year's Day
- Makha Bucha Day
- Chakri Day
- Songkran Festival
- Coronation Day
- Visakha Bucha Day
- Asahna Bucha Day
- H.M. Queen's Birthday
- Chulalongkorn Day (Rama V Day)
- H.M. King's Birthday
- Constitution Day
- New Year's Eve.
- Songkran and Coronation Day fall in the main holiday.
- Chulalongkorn Day falls in the October break.

So that's another 10 holidays, which means that you work 9 a.m to 3 p.m. five days a week for 38 weeks and enjoy 14 weeks vacation. In Thailand.

CHAPTER 16: WHAT DOES IT COST TO LIVE IN THAILAND?

My $2.00 lunch: ginger chicken, steamed vegetables, rice

My $7.50 Day

When I'm working I try to keep a steady routine and a simple diet. I thought you might find it interesting to see something of what's available here (of course everything's available at a price) and what it costs to eat out three meals a day.

The photo above is my breakfast: rice congee (porridge) with pork balls, fresh scallions, ginger, and topped with crisp noodles. Served at one of Chiang Mai's oldest family restaurants. With a 500 ml. of bottled water to wash it down, the bill is $1.50. I usually tip 15¢, which elicits a lovely wai, the Thai bow with hands clasped over the heart and, of course, a big smile.

Then off to my 'office', the Mamia Coffee Shop on the bank of the River Ping, where the staff prepares a gigantic iced coffee frappe, below, as soon as I arrive. That's $2.10. Later they'll make me lunch: ginger chicken and savory vegetables with steamed rice ($2.00, above), which I eat while watching the river (currently in flood and quite exciting) flow by.

Evenings, having had enough cooked food and animal protein, I head into town for a fruit or vegetable smoothie, as you see being prepared below. If it's fruit, they'll blend the juice and flesh of a ripe coconut with 4 passion fruit and two ripe bananas. If it's vegetables, into the blender goes another coconut along with a football-sized avocado. Pretty simple. Pretty cheap: $1.70 for either one. The staff here practices the ancient Thai art of fruit-carving – spectacularly beautiful flowers and dragons created out of melons – when business is slow.

So that's an average day of healthy eating. With tips it comes to $7.50. Eating out for a month – 90 meals – costs me $225.00. If I wanted to prepare the same meals at home my monthly food bill would be about $130.

Living on a Budget

I cover this in great detail in *How to Retire in Thailand and Double Your Income*, but here's a quick look at your basic budget. Remember, there are other costs, like medical insurance, that need to be considered too.

RENTAL	THAI BAHT	US $
House	8,000 – 50,000	275 – 1,700
Apartment	5,000 – 20,000	170 – 650
Flat or Room	2,000 – 10,000	70 – 350
UTILITIES		
Elec., Apartment (landlord)	1,000 – 5,000	35 - 75
Electric, house	1,000 – 2,000	35 - 80
Water (landlord)	200 – 1,000	70 - 30
Water (direct)	100 – 400	3 – 15
FOOD	5,000 – 10,000	170 – 350
TRANSPORTATION		
Walk, bike, songthaew, taxi	2,000 – 3,000	70 – 100
Rented moped	2,500 – 3,500	85 – 120
Own car	3,000 – 5,000	100 – 170
ENTERTAINMENT		
Nightlife, weekends	2,000 – 5,000	200 – 300

Nightlife, five days	10,000 – 20,000	500 - 850
Cable TV	500 – 1,000	18 – 40
Internet Cafe	200 – 500	7 – 18
Internet 1 Mb.	500 – 600	18 – 20
MAID, Live-In	5,000 – 10,000	170 - 350

CHAPTER 17: LANGUAGE BOOKS AND COURSES

If you're keen to get started right away, here are some of the best books on the subject:

Learn The Thai Alphabet in one Day: It allows you to master the mysterious Thai script. It's not an alphabet but an abugida, a writing system in which each consonant may invoke an inherent vowel sound, described as an implied 'a' or 'o'. Download this jewel for $12.99. It lives up to its title.

Pimsleur Language Programs: Pimsleur Language Programs are well established and effective. If you're a learning by listening person get the Pimsleur audio Learn Thai Language CD's. Listen before you come then, when you get to Thailand, it will all make sense. (Simon & Schuster. $120). Also used for much less $$ on Amazon.

Colloquial Thai: Covers the language that all the other books miss. Thai slang and idioms that 'official' books often miss. Surprise your Thai friends with a little slang. Kindle. $22.95

Improving Your Thai Pronunciation: Both a book and an audio CD that increases your ability to pronounce Thai words with more fluency. Audio CD. $10.95

The Lonely Planet Thai Phrase Book: The Lonely Planet Thai Phrasebook is your best Thai friend. You'll use it very day. Amazon $9.

More Thai Language: The Best Thai Movies With Subtitles

Thai movies are an easy way to get acquainted with Thailand, it's culture and it's language. Start by looking for these DVDs on Netflix. There's no easier or more enjoyable way to study Thai language and culture than to watch a classic Thai movie. Here are eight of the best, all with English subtitles:

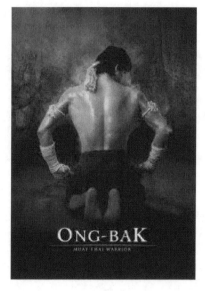

Ong Bak: Muay Thai Warrior. An action film with Tony Jaa as a young villager trying to recover stolen Buddha head. This film enjoyed great popularity in the west and Tony Jaa became a major worldwide celebrity.

Ong Bak 2 and Ong Bak 3: Success breeds sequels or, in this case, prequels. Both of these films take Tony Jaa's character back to the 15th. century when magic was still alive and well. In addition to being enjoyable, well-produced films they give a rich depiction of medieval Thailand - at least as the filmmakers imagined it. Both showcase Tony Jaa as actor and director, enhanced by much bigger budgets.

A Man Called Tone: A sophisticated film with a strong script, fascinating characters, and some of the best acting ever seen in Thai cinema. Thai critics and intellectuals hailed it as proof that Thailand could produce great movies.

The Protector: Another Tony Jaa vehicle: adrenaline-pumping, and high octane Thai movie also starring Tony Jaa. All action, all the time, it is nevertheless both fun to watch and a useful lesson in Thai slang vocabulary.

Monrak Looktung: Magical Love in the Countryside. A charming musical that was made in the 1970's and remade in 2005. A rural love story packed with Thai 'peasant' tunes. Many consider this the high point of 20th. century Thai filmmaking. It ran for over 6 months in theaters throughout Thailand and adds yet another dimension to our appreciation of Thai culture.

Tropical Malady: A romantic double tale of gay love. It was the first Thai film to win the coveted Jury Prize at the Cannes Film Festival. At first it was ignored but Quentin Tarantino's advocacy of it forced critics to take a second, closer look.

Kao Cheu Karn: Thailand's first great advocacy film. It forced the elite and the middle class to take an unflinching look at Thailand's hidden (feudal) problems of corruption and poverty. It's impact on Thai society and subsequently, politics was staggering and persists to this day.

A Different Culture

A British businessman who retired to a beach community here hired some local tradesmen to hang some imported wall-paper in his new house. Wall-paper is unknown in Thailand, and he failed to supervise the workers since the rest of their jobs were of high quality. After the job was done – poorly, by his high standards – he loudly criticized the contractor in front of his crew.

The next day as he was riding home on his moped he was waylaid by the contractor and his brothers, all armed with pick-handles. They beat him unmercifully. He has still not recovered and doctors doubt he ever will.

The Thai police, after concluding their investigation, decided not to prosecute the contractor because in their opinion the two offenses balanced out.

Many expats here were outraged at what they considered a gross miscarriage of justice. But my friend, an Australian professor of Thai culture, told me that the verbal attack and humiliation of the Thai contractor is regarded by Thais the same way we regard 'assault with a deadly weapon', and that his attack on the British businessman was 'fair'.

CHAPTER 18: FORTY REASONS TO LIVE AND WORK IN THAILAND

1. **Culture:** It has taken Thais a thousand years to create a culture devoted to happiness, tolerance, and beauty. All we have to do is enjoy it.

2. **Cost of Living:** If you live on a fixed income, you can double it's buying power just by moving here.

3. **Climate:** Some like it hot, and Thai summers oblige. Some like it warm, Thai winters are wonderful. And there are always the cool mountains and 1,000 km of white, sandy beaches.

4. **Thai Women:** Beautiful, gentle, gracious, and charming. They're hard to beat.

5. **Beaches:** Sure, other countries have beaches, but the hundreds of miles of beaches here are attached to Thailand!

6. **Beer:** Something for every palate: Singha, Leo, Chang, Tiger, Phuket, Klassik, the list goes on. And served over ice.

7. **Martial arts:** Unique, fast-moving, Muay Thai draws enthusiasts from around the world.

8. **Flowers:** Orchids grow wild everywhere. And orchids are just the beginning of Thailand's floral glory. You could spend a lifetime on the flowers alone.

9. **Jungles:** Thailand's jungles are fascinating: filled with flowers, animals, and exotic tribal people, all within a day's walk of bars serving cold beer.

10. **Ethnic Diversity:** Thailand is home to a wonderful variety of people each with a unique history, cuisine, costume, and sense of humor. A lifetime's study and delight.

11. **Nursing, Medical and Dental Care:** Many people live in Thailand primarily because of the quality of its medical care!

12. **Shopping:** From banana leaves spread out on the pavement at dawn to gigantic, European hypermarkets, Thailand offers an unparalleled variety of inexpensive shopping experiences.

13. **Smiles:** Thais' smiles came 1,000 years before the tourist slogan. The tourists might leave, but the smiles won't.

14. **Night Life:** If you like fireworks at 2 a.m., dancing, singing, music, and cold beer, Thailand is heaven.

15. **Safety:** Women and children can walk the streets more safely here, day or night, than almost any place on earth.

16. **History:** A unique and wildly divergent amalgam of myth, legend, and cultures, Thai history offers a lifetime of study. Never colonized. No 'colonial cringe'. (They're not really interested in learning your language).

17. **Festivals:** Like dressing up? Blowing things up? Setting things on fire? Singing? Dancing? Rowing? Looking at flowers? Dousing people with water? Thailand has a festival just for you. As I was coming to work this morning traffic was held up for miles to make room for a giant, wild-looking dragon snaking down the middle of the highway. Thousands of people will be late for work. Great!

18. **Restaurants and Speakeasies:** They're literally everywhere: in carports, under houses, on vacant lots, in alleys, streets, on rivers, mountains, in temples. And every one has their own idea of how to prepare food. Nobody cooks at home here. Want to sell whisky by the roadside? Go ahead!

19. **Things to Do:** From hot springs to transvestite night clubs, Thais find room in their hearts, minds, wallets, and schedules for just about every form of human diversion.

21. Animism + Hinduism + Buddhism + Christianity + Confucianism?: There's room in Thailand for all of them. Even mixed together. Even in one person! Imagine the fun of seeing them all alive and well in one place, at one time.

22. The weather: T-shirt, shorts, flip flops all year round. When the temperature drops below 70F Thais bundle up and enjoy shivering. Too hot? Head for the hills or camp out on Thailand's 3,200 km of beautiful beaches.

23. Tipping: Taxi drivers are ecstatically happy with a 30 cent tip.

24. World's most varied coffee shops: Riverside? Mountain top? Local coffee? Transvestite coffee shops serving imported organic coffee? We've got you covered.

25. Store clerks wai you for buying a carton of milk: Transactions begin and end with a bow and a blessing. What's not to like about that?

26. Noodle carts are considered part of the traffic flow: Five lanes of rush hour traffic + one guy pushing a noodle cart, at night, without lights? No problem!

27. Entertainment: Cable TV has 6 English-language channels, plus German, French, Vietnamese and Chinese. There are movieplexes, festivals, and holidays, including one (Loy Krathong) devoted to setting things on fire and floating them into the sky!

28. "Traffic" is an excuse for anything: Thais' politeness is matched only by their lack of punctuality. That's why "traffic" is so handy.

29. You're More Interesting than an Elephant: In many parts of Thailand children will literally topple over as they watch you go by. Finally, you're getting the attention you always wanted.

30. The Language: Written Thai is not an alphabet and spoken Thai depends on tones as much as on syllables. Learning it opens a new window on the world.

31. **Fresh Mango with Sticky Rice:** Thailand's gift to civilization. Fall in love with food all over again...for 60¢.

32. **Temples on Every Block:** Sometimes two or three. And talk about exotic! You can sit and boggle for hours. I see a new one, always unique, every few days.

33. **Thai Women Really Forgive and Forget:** Heartbreak? Disappointment? Betrayal? Thai women can (after the initial knife-wielding onslaught, of course) just drop it completely and move on.

34. **Transportation:** Limo? Air train? Taxi? Pedicab? Tuktuk? Songtaew? Bus? Plane? Train? Scooter? You name it, it's affordable and it's waiting for you.

35. **Accommodation:** Modern Thai houses are cool, sturdy, and airy. Traditional ones are beautiful and built of rosewood and teak. And cheap.

36. **Fighting:** Cock-fights, cricket fights, kite fights, guy-fights, gal-fights and the foreigners' favorite: bar-fights. Yep, we've got 'em all.

37. **Freedom:** could learn a lot...Seriously, you're free to do almost anything you can think of so long as you don't harm anyone else. In Thailand, you'll discover what "unregulated" really means.

38. **Happy, Laughing Drunks:** Fights are rare. Laughs are plentiful. Most nights people sit around outdoors drinking beer, but apart from a lot of giggling and some singing, that's about it.

39. **Wonderful drivers:** Regardless of freaked-out foreigners' opinions, you'll find that Thais are extremely considerate, patient, and skilled drivers.

40. **Re-set Yourself:** Thailand is so exotic, so different, and so
beautiful that it literally re-sets our minds, bodies, and hearts. It takes
us out of ourselves and our concerns and allows us "time out" to
reconsider life.

RESOURCES FOR THAILAND ENTREPRENEURS

Websites, Blogs, Search Engine Optimization, etc.
Ryan Mendenhall. mendenhallcreative@gmail.com

For General Questions and Introductions, write me:
godfree@gmail.com

ABOUT THE AUTHOR

If you're a fellow victim of the financial crisis you know that life has handed us a lemon right at the end of our working lives. The trick is to make lemonade with it.

(I grew up in Australia, lived in Japan, then got my doctorate at UMass, Amherst, started several US companies and lived an enjoyable life, including regular visits to Paris for the French Open. The financial crisis wiped me out. I'm now 72 and enjoying life more than ever, to my great surprise).

I've found that it really is possible to live in comfort and beauty on $1,200 a month – something that seemed impossible when I was expelled from the middle-class five years ago. I lost my business and my lovely 5-acre California home and was left with nothing but my Social Security, which had seemed so insignificant before that I never noticed it.

After paying off my employees I had nothing left but my furniture and household appliances. So I sold all of it on eBay and set off around the world to find a place where:

1. I could live comfortably on my Social Security and
2. I could make enough extra money to restore my fortunes.

I did, and it's Thailand. In Thailand my $1200/mo. Social Security check immediately allowed me to rejoin the middle class. The extra money I've made since then has already got me thinking about going to next year's French Open. If you want to stay up to date, email me at godfree@thailandretirementhelpers.com and I'll send you our newsletter.

21079612R00063

Made in the USA
Columbia, SC
14 July 2018